Filled With His Glory

Filled With His GLORY

A Journey into the Spirit-filled Life

ALETHA HINTHORN

Beacon Hill Press of Kansas City
Kansas City, Missouri

ISBN 083-411-8238

Printed in the
United States of America

Cover Design: Marie Tabler

Library of Congress Cataloging-in-Publication Data

Hinthorn, Aletha.
Filled with His glory : a journey into the spirit-filled life / Aletha Hinthorn.
p. cm.
ISBN 0-8341-1823-8
1. Christian life—Biblical teaching. I. Title.
BS680.C47H55 1999
248.4—dc21
99-40432
CIP

10 9 8 7 6 5 4 3 2 1

Contents

Foreword

Aletha Hinthorn's study of the main furnishings of Israel's ancient Tabernacle radiates her passion to know God, a passion that should fill every Christian. She takes the reader through the compartments of the Tabernacle, stopping chapter by chapter to discuss the items of furniture in order. Each item, built at God's instruction to God's specifications, taught ancient Israel important truth about His character and about the nature and necessity of holiness for the one who would worship the holy God. Each item continues to be significant; each has much to teach the modern believer who is willing to learn.

Ms. Hinthorn's purpose is not to give a detailed description of the materials, the construction, or the use of the various Tabernacle furnishings she includes in this study. That has been done many times already. Rather, she intends to help the reader understand and incorporate the lessons of the Tabernacle—God's dwelling in ancient Israel—into his or her own life and into our lives together as the community of faith in Christ. Each piece, from the altar of sacrifice to the ark of the covenant, foreshadowed an important element of Jesus' life and sacrifice for us. In turn, we can—if we will—find each piece of the Tabernacle furnishings replicated in spiritual meaning as we continue further in our walk with God.

A word of encouragement is in order here. This is a legitimate method of Bible study. It has been neglected and even scoffed at by some in recent years as biblical studies have advanced, as though methods used as long ago as the church fathers could hardly be useful for our modern (or even postmodern) age. But it remains legitimate. Often it is called the typological approach: a person, a place, an event, or, as in this study, the furnishings of Israel's ancient Tabernacle pointed to greater realities beyond themselves, into the future of God's redemptive purpose and plan. They are said to be "types," finding their fulfillment in something greater still to come. A simpler way to understand this concept is simply to realize that, in some cases, ancient realities could and did become symbols of later and greater realities.

Three observations confirm that this approach can be valid. First, in the Old Testament God often took familiar things and used them to teach Israel new truth. For example, God's covenant with Israel used a covenant treaty form that was widely known at that time in the ancient Near East. Another example: the floor plan of the Tabernacle had been used in sanctuaries in the Near East for at least 2,000 years before Moses' day; God was simply reclaiming the architectural plan to its rightful use and rightful Owner!

Second, some of the New Testament writers used this method. Paul taught that Abraham's son Ishmael was a "type" (symbol) of the Law given at Mount Sinai, while Isaac was the fulfillment of God's specific promise to Abraham and a "type" (symbol) of the grace found in Jesus Christ. The author of Hebrews called the Tabernacle "a symbol for the present time . . . [of] the greater and more perfect tabernacle, not made with hands" (9:9, 11, NASB).

Third, this really is the recognition of a particular kind of metaphor. A metaphor is the comparison of two things that are alike in (usually only) one point, so the thing compared becomes a symbol, in that one point, of the thing to which it is being compared. For example, "He is a rock" usually is an admiring comment on a person's steadfastness, reliability, or loyalty, not a putting down of his appearance or intelligence. One of the really important and solid advances in biblical studies in recent decades has been the increasing recognition of the importance of metaphor in the Bible as one of the ways by which God revealed himself and His plan of redemption in and through Jesus Christ.

The Old Testament Tabernacle (later, Solomon's Temple) and its furnishings, as well as many other items and even some persons, places, and events in Old Testament history, can work this way too. They were real in and of themselves, and we dare not forget that if we wish to be faithful Bible interpreters. But just as a rock may remind us of a person's admirable quality of steadiness, so the ancient altar of sacrifice taught and teaches that sin must be dealt with; the table of shewbread taught and teaches that God desires to feed us richly; the ark of the covenant taught and teaches that ultimately God acted to make it possible for all to enter into His presence. As Ms. Hinthorn reminds us, "God first teaches us abstract truths through concrete forms."

Two notes of caution are also in order. First, it would be a mistake for anyone to think that this is the only method of Bible study, or even that it should be used by itself without regard for other methods. I can assure the reader that this is the farthest thing from Ms. Hinthorn's intention. This particular kind of biblical metaphor is real, and it is important. Where it occurs, it should be noticed and studied. But it is not all that can and should be noticed in our Bible study, even in those passages where it has much to teach us.

Second, this method of Bible study must be used with strict controls. We cannot make up our own "types." Only where the Bible itself already has indicated that something in the Old Testament is to be regarded as a type of Christ, of Christ's work, or of some aspect of the Christian life and walk may we follow the Bible's lead and interpret along those lines. This Ms. Hinthorn has done well. She interprets and expounds on the significance of only what the Bible (particularly in the Book of Hebrews) already has identified as having typological, as well as literal, meaning.

There is an important reason for this caution. We could invent—and many interpreters, both ancient and modern, have invented—a great number of fanciful, silly, and sometimes even dangerous "types" if all we have are our own imaginations as a control upon the method. Without this restraint, everything in the Old Testament soon becomes a type and only a type, and interpreters compete with each other to come up with the greatest number, and the most original, of typological interpretations.

These cautions are needed here only because so many in the past have abused this tool of Bible study, a tool that is legitimate if used when and how it should be used. Ms. Hinthorn has used this tool, this method, properly, for the New Testament itself teaches that the Tabernacle was a type of the permanent things to come in Christ, as well as being the real worship center of ancient Israel. As God taught ancient Israel to worship in the real Tent, so a correct understanding of that Tent's symbolic significance has much to teach the modern believer about God's greater purposes fulfilled in Christ, and the holy life to which we are called in Christ.

Aletha Hinthorn has done the Church a signal service in explaining the symbolism of the ancient Tabernacle furnishings and exhorting the Christian to take its meaning to heart. May God bless you richly as you follow her lead through this series of studies.

—Joseph Coleson
Professor of Old Testament
Nazarene Theological Seminary
Kansas City

Preface

THE CALL to write this book came after months during which I pled with the Lord to allow me to give Him glory. I recognized I could satisfy that deep hunger only by calling people to holiness.

About the same time, a friend made a comment comparing the Old Testament Tabernacle to the dwelling place Christ wants to have within us. This stirred within my spirit a longing to study the Tabernacle. As I studied, I found holiness was the theme of both the Old Testament Book of Exodus and of His holy dwelling.

Yet I saw more than God's call for us to be holy. I saw His passionate longing to rest in us. He was not calling His people to be holy because He's a pharisaical God demanding that His people maintain a certain standard. Rather, He's a loving God who can be satisfied only if we're near Him. Through the study, I began to hear the yearning in the final line of Jesus' last recorded prayer on earth: "that I myself may be in them" (John 17:26).

I heard, "Be holy, so I can fill you to overflowing with My presence, My joy. Unless you're holy, I cannot reveal myself to you."

My heart began to cry with Moses, "Show me Your glory" (Exod. 33:18, AMP.). The Septuagint gives the essence of his plea: "Show me thyself."

Moses' longing has been fulfilled. "We beheld his glory" (KJV), John exclaimed. "The Word became flesh and made his dwelling among us. We have seen his glory" (John 1:14).

The phrase "made his dwelling" means Jesus "tabernacled" among us (AMP.). He became the true dwelling place for the presence of God. When we look closely, though, we find that the pattern God gave Moses of the

Tabernacle was more than a design that was perfectly fulfilled in Christ. It is the design for the spirits of all those who say with Moses, "Show me Your glory."

If we want God's glory to fill our spiritual temples, we must follow the pattern God gave Moses on the mountain. As soon as Moses completed the work, God's glory so filled the Tabernacle that Moses could not enter. When the Holy Spirit takes full possession of us, we, too, find there is no room for self.

We are *all for His glory!*

God had one purpose when He formed Adam. He wanted to create a happy people.[1] Ultimate happiness rests in Him, so He made this offer: I will come inside you and give you My fullness—fullness of joy!

How would He tell us to prepare for His indwelling? He chose to give the plan for His dwelling place on earth, the Tabernacle, to the Israelites. Only later would His people understand that "we are His temple."

Introduction

"YOU are in me, and I am in you" (John 14:20).

"I in them and you in me" (17:23).

Jesus' words were full of holy mystery. "How will this be . . . ?" we ask with Mary, the mother of Jesus (Luke 1:34). God has nothing greater to tell us than of our dwelling in Him and He in us, and He made ample provision for us to understand both of these concepts.

"You are in me." God teaches us this delightful possibility by letting us picture Canaan, the land He promised the Israelites when they left Egypt.

"I am in you." God also gave a preview of His dwelling in us in the story of the Tabernacle: "Then have them make a sanctuary for me, and I will dwell among them" (Exod. 25:8).

The story of the Tabernacle is the story of Christ in us. In each piece of furniture we see Christ and His ministry in our lives, and we also see what God requires of us. From the altar of burnt offerings to the ark of the covenant, God teaches His provision for us to move from surrender to being filled with His presence.

His Holy Plan

The pattern of the Tabernacle was so important in God's mind that He spent more time explaining that than He spent telling us about His entire creation. In 2 chapters He describes creation, but He took 50 chapters to tell about the Tabernacle, the place where He would dwell: 13 in Exodus, 18 in Leviticus, 13 in Numbers, 2 in Deuteronomy, and 4 in Hebrews. God's design for His dwelling place *within* us is more important to Him than the creation of the world.

Our Father, who wants us to understand how to build a sanctuary for Him, has given us the design of His dwelling. If a builder wants to understand a future building, he looks at the architect's plan. How much better we can understand spiritual realities through carefully examining the plan the Holy Spirit gives in the Tabernacle.

In this study, we will be considering only a few aspects of the seven pieces of furniture within the Tabernacle and the outer court. When the Israelites came to worship at the Tabernacle, the first piece they approached was the altar of burnt offering, sometimes called the brazen altar—so our study will begin with this piece. We come as worshipers.

The altar of burnt offering teaches us to empty ourselves of self so we can be filled with His glory.

The laver is the place of continual washing. Jesus said we as believers are "clean because of the word I have spoken to you" (John 15:3).

The lampstand assures us of continual light and grace.

The table of the bread of the Presence invites us to enjoy communion with the Lord.

The golden altar of incense is our place of worship and intercession.

The atonement cover reminds us that the precious blood of Jesus covers all sin.

The ark of the covenant speaks of God's holy presence within us.

Before we consider the spiritual significance of individual furniture pieces, let's look at the overall structure of the Tabernacle. Every detail displayed spiritual implications of our Lord Jesus Christ and also of the dwelling we are to prepare within us. "As he is, so are we" (1 John 4:17, KJV).

Notice that when God looked on the Tabernacle, He saw in the arrangement of the furniture the shape of the Cross.

God told Moses, "See to it that you make everything according to the pattern shown you on the mountain" (Heb. 8:5). It is just as important for us to follow the pat-

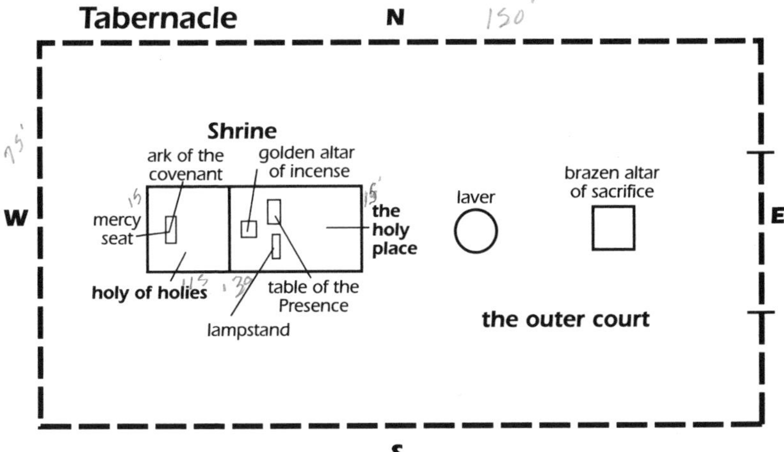

tern God gave for His dwelling as it was for Moses. In this book we'll explore the temple He desires to inhabit and look at the provisions He has made for His life in us.

Using This Book

The questions in this study are of two types. One type asks that you look up and record what Scripture says. This is not to be done merely as an exercise, but as a listener who wants to better understand. The Hebrew word for "manna" means "what is it?" because those words sound like what the Israelites said when they saw the manna on the ground. Before God's Word can become manna to us, we, too, must ask, "What is it? What is it to me? What does it mean for my life?" When we're eager to know, God gives us understanding, and His Word becomes bread for our spirits.

The second type of question aims to help you apply biblical truth. Participation among those in your group should be optional for all questions, but especially for those requiring a personal response.

Be willing to share what the Holy Spirit teaches you. Samuel Logan Brengle, one of the great leaders of the Salvation Army, believed in sharing his own personal experience: "I look upon God's dealings with my soul, not as something to be hidden in my own heart for my personal comfort and guidance, but as a trust for the tempted and hungry-hearted who will hear and read me."[1] God will make you a channel of His blessings as you share His work in your life.

To simplify the material, we have organized it into three parts:

- The Old Testament Presentation—a brief description as God gave it to Moses
- Fulfilled in Christ—a brief description of the Old Testament shadow we see fulfilled in Christ
- Fulfilled in Us—the remainder of the chapters

My prayer is that He will reveal His glory to you until a longing to be filled with His glory captivates your entire spirit.

God has chosen our spirits to be His dwelling place!

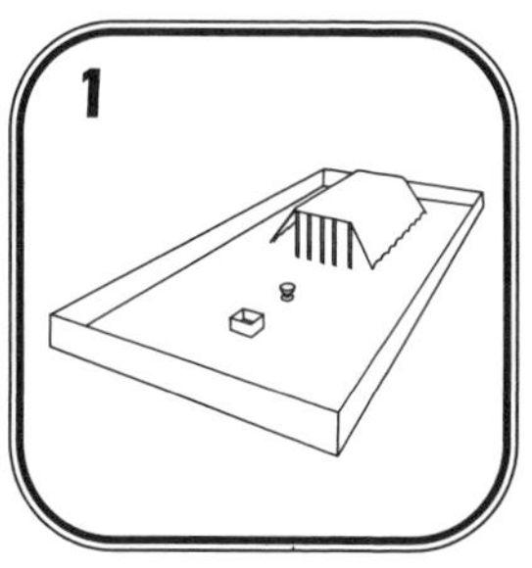

The Temple He Wants to Fill

"PROCESS this through your spirit," a Christian speaker said as she shared ideas she thought our group might be reluctant to receive. Would we listen with our hearts as well as our intellects?

Most Americans value becoming strong intellectually or physically but don't seek to become strong in spirit. Yet Jesus became "strong in spirit" (Luke 2:40, KJV), and in this world we are to be like Him (see 1 John 4:17). This is the first concept we need to understand as we begin to prepare God's tabernacle—His dwelling place within us.

God is Spirit, and our communion with Him is through our spirits. Some years ago I had an experience that gave me a deep respect for spiritual realities. In closing my prayer times, I began telling the Lord I wanted my spirit to commune with His Spirit. Often I experienced a profound sense of being strengthened in my spirit.

One day as I sat quietly before the Lord, He was suddenly there. As I saw Him with my spirit (my eyes were closed), I was overwhelmed with His reality. The chair by which I was kneeling and everything around me seemed unreal, like a shadow, compared to Him. At a very deep level I knew God, who is Spirit, to be the real One.

The spiritual becomes more apparent to us as we seek to become spiritually sensitive. In *The Chronicles of Narnia,* by C. S. Lewis, Lucy told her friends that she was going to follow Aslan the lion. The others could not see him, but on Lucy's word they began following what she said was Aslan. As they followed, Aslan became increasingly visible to them.[1]

That's the way it is with us spiritually. Things of the Spirit become more real as we study His Word and seek to follow His still, small voice.

Become Strong in Spirit

"God is the absolutely real one; when He enters a person's life, it is we who are suddenly aware of our tentative and fragile existence," wrote William Dyrness.[2] The temptation, though, is to regard the visible as more real than the spiritual or the invisible. Consider the following points to strengthen your spiritual awareness.

1. Paul cautions, "We fix our eyes not on what is seen, but on what is unseen. For what is seen is temporary, but what is unseen is eternal" (2 Cor. 4:18). Restate this verse in your own words.

2. What does it mean to have your eyes fixed on something? Apply this to your spiritual eyes.

3. "And the child [John the Baptist] grew and became strong in spirit" (Luke 1:80). Just as John the Baptist, who prepared the way for Christ to come, was strong in spirit, so we, too, must learn to become strong in spirit as we prepare the way for Christ to come in new ways to our hearts. Reflect on what you think it means to be strong in spirit. Consider the definition of "spiritual" in Gal. 6:1 in the *Am-*

plified Bible: "you who are spiritual [who are responsive to and controlled by the Spirit]."

4. We know God by the impression of His Spirit upon our spirits. See 1 Cor. 2:11-12.

5. What evidences do Rom. 8:14-16 and 1 Cor. 2:12-15 give that the Holy Spirit communicates with our spirits?

6. All Christians can be spiritually discerning. How does John 10:27 state that Jesus was confident our spirits could discern what the Spirit of God wants to teach us?

In *The Last Battle,* in the *Chronicles of Narnia,* the children were leaving Narnia, the shadowlands, and going to the forever land. Their reflections on the land they were leaving may resemble our thoughts when we enter heaven and reflect on our earthly life. As the children looked back, they recognized that all they had left was like a shadow compared with the realities ahead of them. Lucy and Lord Digory tried to describe the forever land.

"'More like the real thing,' said the Lord Digory softly. . . . 'And of course it is different; as different as a real thing is from a shadow or as waking life is from a dream.'"[3]

C. S. Lewis's words sound a bit like those of the writer to the Hebrews when he described the Old Testament Tabernacle as "a shadow of the good things to come" (10:1, NKJV). The Tabernacle was a copy of the spiritual building God wants to form within each of us.

Spiritual ideas can seem vague, though, so God first teaches us abstract truths through concrete forms. "The spiritual did not come first, but the natural, and after that the spiritual" (1 Cor. 15:46). So it is with God's plan for the Tabernacle: first He gives the physical pattern, then the spiritual.

God's Passion to Indwell Our Spirits

God gave us the Tabernacle pattern to help us prepare our spirits to be His dwelling. Moses first built the Tabernacle, and Solomon later built the Temple as a dwelling place for God.

After Solomon built the Temple, he wondered, "But will God really dwell on earth? The heavens, even the highest heaven, cannot contain you. How much less this temple I have built!" (1 Kings 8:27).

To that we say, "Solomon, if only you could have known! He was coming to dwell within *our* temples—within *us!*"

Jesus said, "The kingdom of God is within you" (Luke 17:21).

1. What do the following verses say is God's temple?

1 Cor. 3:16-17

1 Cor. 6:19

2 Cor. 6:16

2. When I read David's words in 1 Chron. 22:1, "The house of the LORD God is to be here," I think, "Yes, here within me!" I hear God saying, "My presence, My fullness, is to be in you!" Write some of your thoughts about this.

God promised His people a place of rest. "The eternal God is your refuge, and underneath are the everlasting arms" (Deut. 33:27). What a place to rest!

Although the truth of resting in the Lord is utterly delightful, consider this more awesome truth: not only has God come to give us rest, but also *He has come to rest in us!*

God asked, "Where is the house you will build for me? Where will my resting place be?" (Isa. 66:1; see also Acts 7:48-49). We're amazed that God, who is never weary nor sleeps, desires a place in which to dwell. However, His choice for a dwelling is even more remarkable.

"For the LORD has chosen Zion, he has desired it for his [habitation, KJV]: 'This is my resting place for ever and ever; here I will sit enthroned, for I have desired it'" (Ps. 132:13-14).

In Christian thought, Zion refers to the Church.[4] Repeatedly God tells us that He has chosen us, His people, to be His resting-place. For instance, see Ps. 76:2 and Joel 3:21.

3. The concept of God's dwelling place is seen throughout Scripture. How do the following references restate this truth?

Eph. 2:22

Heb. 3:6

4. Read these verses in Exodus, and record the different statements God made expressing His purpose for the Tabernacle.

Exod. 29:42-46

Exod. 30:6

5. In Exod. 25:8, what did God promise to do for His people? What was their responsibility?

In Eph. 3:17, Paul prayed that Christ might "dwell in your hearts." When discussing this verse, Roger Hahn, professor of New Testament at Nazarene Theological Seminary in Kansas City, illustrates with the following incident what it means for God to dwell in our hearts. When he and his wife, Dorothy, pastored in Florida, Dorothy told some overnight guests, "Make yourselves at home."

The next morning when the Hahns entered the living room, one of their guests was up and sitting comfortably with his feet on the coffee table. The guest's wife said, "Oh, Honey—don't put your feet there," to which he replied, "Dorothy said for me to make myself at home."

"That's what it means for Christ to dwell in us," Dr. Hahn said. "He is free to come in and be at home in us."

If God is at home within us, He's free to do what He wants. He may want to write someone an encouraging note or to give someone a hug or to send a check to a single mom. He may want to give us a spirit of prayer while we're driving to work. If He's at home within us, we respond to His inner promptings to love rather than to criticize, to forgive rather than to remember a wrong.

6. How does it make you feel to know that God wants to dwell with you? What pictures or concepts does the thought "I am His resting-place" bring to you? Consider the new perspective this truth gives to Phil. 4:13.

7. "That I myself may be in them" (John 17:26) was not only Jesus' final prayer but also His repeated longing. Why do you think Jesus so frequently spoke of living in us? For examples, see John 14:20; 17:21-23.

8. God appears to interchangeably use His resting in us and our resting in Him. We are at rest in Him when He is at rest in us. See John's words in 1 John 4:12-15.

9. Reread Ps. 132:13-14, and list at least three truths these verses teach about God and His resting-place.

a.

b.

c.

10. God repeats a thought not (as we do) because He can't think of a fresh idea. What concept did He repeat? Why do you think He said it twice?

11. God emphasizes that He desires to be at rest in Zion—in us! "This is my resting place for ever and ever; here I will sit enthroned, for I have desired it" (Ps. 132:14). God comes eagerly! If He desires to dwell with us, should

we not allow it to happen? What does God's eagerness to indwell us say about the value He places upon us?

12. What joy we find in the thought that God eagerly desires to dwell within us! Pause and let God speak this truth to your spirit now.

God Dwells in a Holy Place

Jesus' desire to indwell us echoed the yearning God revealed after He delivered His people out of Egypt. He wanted them to experience more than deliverance from bondage; He wanted to continually dwell with them. "Then have them make a sanctuary for me, and I will dwell among them" (Exod. 25:8).

In Exod. 10, Pharaoh suggested different compromises to avoid a total separation, but Moses understood the Israelites could not build God's dwelling as long as they remained in Egypt.

1. We, too, must be completely delivered from sin before we can know God's abiding presence. Look for the command that closely follows the promise "I will dwell in them" in 2 Cor. 6:16-17, KJV.

2. When our Creator God says that nothing but complete separation from sin satisfies Him, how foolish we are to argue! Satan still tries to hinder those who want to worship by telling them that they don't need to leave the land

of sin completely behind them. Compare Satan's message today with that of Pharaoh's in Exod. 8:28.

We should listen to our Creator. According to an article in a local newspaper several years ago, a man entered the Nelson Art Gallery and informed the curator that one picture was upside down. Although no one agreed with him, he insisted the picture needed to be changed. Finally someone asked him, "How do you know the picture is upside down?"

"I'm the artist," he replied.

3. God always wanted to have intimate fellowship with us, and the Israelites recognized that to meet with God brought the highest possible happiness. According to Ps. 15, what is required for us to have this highest happiness?

4. Read the description in the following verses of those who live in His presence.

Matt. 5:8

Heb. 12:14

5. Why do you think a lack of holiness hinders us from seeing God?

"I live in a high and holy place, but also with him who is contrite and lowly in spirit" (Isa. 57:15). It is as though God is saying, "Whatever else you understand about the place where I'll be at home, know that it must be a holy place."

"Holiness adorns your house for endless days, O LORD," the psalmist writes in 93:5; and we add, "How lovely is your dwelling place, O LORD Almighty!" (84:1). In fact, holiness is God's only attribute described with the word "beauty"—"Worship the LORD in the beauty of holiness" (29:2, KJV).

Memorize: I pray that out of his glorious riches he may strengthen you with power through his Spirit in your inner being, so that Christ may dwell in your hearts through faith *(Eph. 3:16-17).*

Prayer: *Dear Lord, in my spirit I come before You. I'm so prone to live as though the things I can see, taste, feel, and touch represent the only reality. You alone, however, are the real One. Teach me to walk in the Spirit and be taught by the Spirit so that I may discern spiritual truths.*

I long to prepare my spirit to be Your holy dwelling. Yet at moments I realize that what was prophesied of Jesus could be spoken of me: "They esteemed Him not." Help me to recognize the awesome privilege of being Your resting-place. Come and be at rest in me. Be at rest in my family. I thank You in Jesus' name for delighting in me as Your resting-place. Amen.

Before we can be all for God's glory, we must willingly surrender the rights to our own glory.

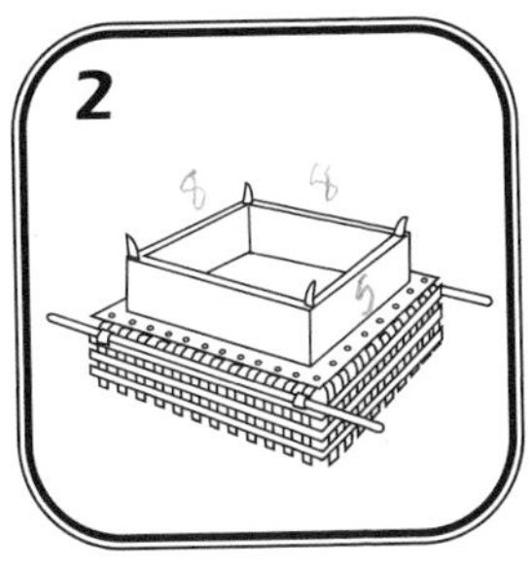

The Altar of Burnt Offering

Read Exod. 27:1-8; 38:1-7.

The outer court had two brass-covered pieces of furniture: the brazen altar and the laver. Brass speaks to us of God's judgment. Outside of the Tabernacle God deals with sin and uncleanness; inside He reveals His glory as He communes with us.

The altar of sacrifice was a hollow chest of acacia wood overlaid with brass. It had horns at the corners and a ledge halfway down. Below the ledge was a grating on all sides.[1]

When the Israelites' offering satisfied God, His fire appeared on the brazen altar: "Fire came out from the presence of the Lord and consumed the burnt offering and the fat portions on the altar. And when all the people saw it, they shouted for joy and fell facedown" (Lev. 9:24).

Fulfilled in Christ

The brazen altar stood at the entrance of the Tabernacle, teaching us that Christ's sacrifice stands at the entrance of all our communion with God. "Without the shedding of blood there is no forgiveness" (Heb. 9:22). Because Jesus offered himself as our sacrifice, we have access to God's dwelling place and presence.

The high priest, the sacrifice, and the altar all have their fulfillment in our crucified Christ. "Then I saw a

Lamb, looking as if it had been slain. . . . And they sang a new song: 'You are worthy to take the scroll and to open its seals, because you were slain, and with your blood you purchased men for God'" (Rev. 5:6, 9).

Fulfilled in Us

The surrender at the brazen altar results in a transformed life. This is where we move from finding our joy in pleasing ourselves to finding our joy in pleasing God.

From the time he was a boy, our son Gregg had dreamed of owning a successful business. One spring his company seemed doomed to failure. God had given him some success, but the business took a downturn. It was not what he had anticipated, and his dreams appeared to be ashes.

Although he had several employees, the question came to him, "Are you willing to work by yourself the rest of your life if God receives more glory through your having a small business rather than a large, successful one?"

After much prayer, Gregg responded, "Yes, Lord—if this is what You want, I'm willing. I want to be God's man more than I want to be successful. If You will receive more glory from my working in this office by myself the rest of my life, I'm willing."

Gregg had yielded personal control of his dreams to God. God knew he meant it, and suddenly Gregg knew God accepted his offering. Despair turned to overwhelming joy.

His circumstances changed slowly, but Gregg was changed dramatically. A few days ago his wife, Sarah, commented there has been as much difference in Gregg since that moment of surrender as there often is when one first becomes a Christian. Sarah is correct—the difference after surrender is great. Gregg is discovering that his joy stems not from a huge response to his advertising campaigns but from his own response to Scripture.

God is looking for those who find their delight in His

commands. When we can say, as my mother said, "If God is pleased, all is well," then we rise to a new level of Christian life.

To be like Christ is to have the one desire He had: "Father, glorify your name!" God could not refrain from responding to such a longing: "I have glorified it, and will glorify it again" (John 12:28). No words could have satisfied Jesus more.

Why would we want to offer ourselves as a living sacrifice, to die with Christ? For the same reason Jesus did: "For the joy set before him [Jesus] endured the cross, scorning its shame" (Heb. 12:2). The joy set before Him was accomplishing His Father's will.

"I delight to do Your will," Jesus could say to His Father (Ps. 40:8, AMP.; see Heb. 10:7). All those who live for His glory find that to be the theme of their hearts. Delighting in His will, finding our joy in knowing that He is pleased, is what it means to be crucified to self.

In this chapter we will discover what happens at the altar where we're crucified with Christ; we'll find out what Paul meant when he said, "I no longer live" (Gal. 2:20).

The Altar—a Place of Suffering

The altar was not a place of beauty but a place of suffering. There was no incense with the animal sacrifices at the brazen altar. Death is never pleasant. If only we could skip this place of sacrifice where we must offer up ourselves to God. However, the altar was "at the door" (Lev. 4:7, KJV). There was no way to approach God without passing this place of sacrifice.

Our natural inclination is not to go there, and we say, "If it be possible, let this cup pass from me" (Matt. 26:39, KJV). But those who follow Jesus all the way say with Him, "Nevertheless not my will, but thine" (Luke 22:42, KJV). That's the essence of our testimony as we go to the Cross.

I was talking with a friend about the need to always

please God rather than self. I suggested that when she and her husband disagreed, she focus on pleasing God with her attitude rather than on doing what she chose to do.

"That's hard to do," she said. Of course—surrender hardly comes naturally and is seldom possible unless we die to the desire to please ourselves. Yet we must remember that we follow a Lamb, a Lamb on His way to the Cross.

1. In dying to self, we surrender our desire to please ourselves so we can live to please the One who lives within us. After surrender we can say with Paul, "We are not trying to please men but God, who tests our hearts" (1 Thess. 2:4).

If this does not happen, we have an ongoing battle. What phrases in Rom. 7:14-24 does Paul use to describe this battle?

2. Notice Paul's anticipation of deliverance in the first sentence of verse 25.

3. Our natural man wants to say, "Thank You, Jesus, for dying for me. But now I want to live my life as I please and accept Your forgiveness while I have my own way." Paul saw it differently. Repeatedly he referred to Christ's death as being his personal experience, and he says we must allow it to be ours. See Gal. 2:20; 6:14; Phil. 2:5-8.

The brass altar included tools for making sure the sacrifice was consumed. The work was to be thorough. You may feel the Spirit prodding you: "Are you willing for Me to have that relationship? What if I ask you to give up that attitude?"

The Holy Spirit is never vague about His requirements.

He knows exactly the one thing we must surrender in order for Him to have our all. It is not that He wants to deny us pleasure. He wants to know, "Do you love Me more than this?"

Vickie and her boyfriend knelt in our family room, asked Jesus into their hearts, and found the joy of having their sins forgiven. A few months later Vickie learned of the need to surrender entirely and to offer her life as a sacrifice to God. As she prayed, the Holy Spirit examined the sincerity of her offer. Would she be willing not to wear the beautiful wedding dress she had purchased? Vickie said that as a girl she had not had a lot of pretty clothes, and her wedding dress represented what was dearest to her heart.

It was a struggle, but finally the wedding dress was on the altar. If God said not to wear it, she would not. With that surrender, He saw she had offered Him her heart's deepest desire. Vickie knew God accepted her sacrifice and purified her heart. She realized later that He had not forbidden her to wear the dress but had asked if she was *willing* not to wear it. Vickie walked down the aisle in a very sacred ceremony in a surrendered wedding dress.

4. God knows what our "wedding dress" is. For Abraham, it was Isaac, his much-loved son of promise. God was asking Abraham to surrender all his ideas about how He was going to fulfill His promise to bless him.

When Abraham surrendered Isaac, God didn't need to ask, "Now, Abraham, what about that land or those sheep?" God knew Isaac represented Abraham's total surrender. That is always what He seeks. He knows if we surrender what is most dear, He has all of us.

"Now I know that you fear God, because you have not withheld from me your son, your only son" (Gen. 22:12).

Rewrite this verse, inserting what you believe the Holy Spirit would say represents *your* "Isaac." Do you love God more than your "Isaac"?

5. The animal chosen as an offering had to be perfect, because it foreshadowed the sinlessness of Jesus, the true sacrifice. The perfect animal also warns us that God asks that the sacrifice we offer must be "whole," or "with no part left out."[2] For us to be a perfect sacrifice to God means that our whole person must be offered. Every part of our lives—work, recreation, homelife, personal relationships, opinions of others, goals—must all be put on the altar. In what areas do you think people find it most difficult to surrender all rights?

6. Why is surrender necessary before we're filled with the Holy Spirit?

God's Fire Fell

1. When we completely surrender at the altar, we say, "Lord, I want to please You more than I want anything else," and we remain there until the fire of the Holy Spirit purifies our desires. God's holy presence was often seen with fire. For instance, see Isa. 6:3-7 and Acts 2:3.

2. The sacrifice on the altar was to be burned through the night. When only ashes remained, the sacrifice was completed. The Lord really does help us to become only ashes!

Write the phrases from Rom. 6:6-7 that indicate there is a time when the work is complete.

The altar is the place to answer God's question, "Will you surrender all rights?" When you do and tell God you have done so, He accepts your sacrifice and sends His Spirit as fire upon your sacrifice. The offering is accepted, and the Holy Spirit in His fullness moves in. Now it's no longer I who live, but Christ (see Gal. 2:20).

My ambitions, plans, and wishes
At my feet in ashes lay.

Then God's fire upon the altar
Of my heart was set aflame.
I shall never cease to praise Him.
Glory, glory to His name!

—Margaret J. Harris

3. Because fire can destroy what is corrupt, the fire burning on the altar symbolized the purifying Spirit of God. The altar was the place where God promised to meet them. It is important that we stay at the altar until God meets us. Read Gen. 15:8-11, 17, and notice that Abraham stayed with the animal sacrifice until God sent fire.

4. When all is on the altar, when the One prodding every aspect of our being finds no more carnal response,

when we are fully surrendered and desiring only to do God's will, then we can—and must—believe that the Holy Spirit has made us holy. The work is done when we believe. See Acts 15:9.

God is pleased to accept our offering. Then it's His work to make us holy. Before God sets us apart as holy for himself, we must be willing for Him to claim all of us for His own.

I love the song by Ralph E. Hudson that says, "I'll live for Him who died for me. / How happy then my life shall be!" When we discover the joy of doing everything for Him, when joy in our lives is defined by "doing what pleases God," then our joy overflows, and we can even say with Paul, "In all our troubles my joy knows no bounds" (2 Cor. 7:4).

Victory at the Altar

When Jesus said, "It is finished" (John 19:30), I think Satan believed Him. Judging from the lack of discernment Satan's followers have, I suspect he thought, "It's over, and I've won." On the Monday night after Easter, some in the Greek Orthodox Church traditionally gather to tell jokes, commemorating the joke God played on Satan when He raised Jesus from the dead.

When He said, "It is finished," Jesus was triumphantly declaring, "The battle is over! I've won the battle against sin." For us, too, "It is finished" is a glorious cry when we've died to sin.

1. What did Matthew mention as the first thing happening at the moment of Jesus' death? See 27:51.

The New Testament suggests that the veil separating the holy place from the most holy place represented the flesh of Jesus Christ that was torn for us on the Cross. When Jesus cried, "It is finished" (John 19:30), "the curtain of the temple was torn in two from top to bottom" (Matt. 27:51). The way into the holy of holies was opened.

The veil also represents our fleshly life—that carnal self that dies when we consecrate ourselves to God.[3] "Those who belong to Christ Jesus have crucified the sinful nature with its passions and desires" (Gal. 5:24).

2. That enmity against God doesn't allow us to want to do all for His glory. Self wants glory. As long as any self remains within us, we cannot enjoy oneness with Him and the fullness of joy He longs to give us. According to Matt. 5:8 and Heb. 12:14, who will see God?

Death is painful, but when we catch a glimpse of the joy set before us, the joy of being filled with all of God's fullness, of knowing that we fully please Him, we, too, will endure the cross and despise the shame (Heb. 12:2, KJV).

When Jesus approached the Cross, He was alone. That place of yielding all is a very personal matter between you and the Holy Spirit. He eagerly seeks to purify you when your heart says, "Yes, Lord," to His perfect will.

Memorize: Therefore, I urge you, brothers, in view of God's mercy, to offer your bodies as living sacrifices, holy and pleasing to God—this is your spiritual act of worship *(Rom. 12:1).*

Prayer: *Dear Lord, I offer myself to You—my past failures, my future hopes, my self-seeking tendencies. May Your fire consume all desires for self until I live only for Your glory. I want every moment of my life to be a sacrifice pleasing to You.*

You have said that what I put on the altar, You sanctify. I lay myself before You in full surrender. Take me and use me. I trust You to accept my sacrifice and to send Your holy fire to fully purify my heart. May the fire of God burn upon the altar of my heart. In Jesus' name I pray. Amen.

When we look into the brazen laver,
we see our uncleanness and are cleansed.

The Washing of the Word

READ Exod. 30:17-21; 38:8.

The laver, made of acacia wood and covered with brass, was filled with water. It was located just past the brass altar and was to be used only by the priests. This fountain of cleansing consisted of a brass bowl resting on a brass base.

As with the brazen altar, brass stands for judgment. The laver was made out of bronze mirrors, and it was at the laver that the priests not only saw their stains but also had them washed away. The priests washed often at the laver; they dared not enter the Tabernacle with any spot on them.

Fulfilled in Christ

James tells us that if we're to draw near to God, we must cleanse our hands (4:8). The water of the laver reminds us of the Word of God in which we're invited to wash. Through the Word, Jesus provides all we need for purity. "Now ye are clean through the word which I have spoken unto you" (John 15:3, KJV).

"Christ loved the church and gave himself up for her to make her holy, cleansing her by the washing with water through the word, and to present her to himself as a radiant church, without stain or wrinkle or any other blemish, but holy and blameless" (Eph. 5:25-27).

Fulfilled in Us

When I was a sophomore in high school, I made a total surrender to God. During the next few years, though, it seemed I spent more time grieving over my failures than enjoying God's fellowship.

One night I fervently prayed, "Lord, have I truly surrendered all to You? Is there any sin remaining in my heart?"

The Holy Spirit spoke these words: "Your heart is clean." What relief flooded my spirit! But God's next words brought a new focus to my life.

"But you need to learn to obey Me."

I now realize God was saying, "You don't spend enough time at the laver." When Jesus washed the disciples' feet, Peter said, "Not just my feet but my hands and my head as well!" (John 13:9).

Jesus replied, "A person who has had a bath needs only to wash his feet; his whole body is clean" (v. 10). Even after God has purified our hearts so that we can wholeheartedly love Him, we may pick up wrong attitudes as we go through life. If we've been crucified with Christ at the brazen altar, the washing of the Word at the laver will keep us clean.

We are not put on the highway of holiness and given an escalator ride to heaven. God purifies our motives when we surrender all at the brazen altar, but we stay cleansed only as we continually wash at the laver. We must keep coming to the Word.

With this word from the Lord, I understood that to obey Him meant to obey *His Word.* I began reading the Bible, not content just to learn what it said, but to know how to live it.

Let's consider how we find cleansing at the laver.

How Are We Cleansed?

James tells us that if we want God to be near us, we must cleanse our hands (4:8). This cleansing is typified in the brazen laver.

1. Write the phrases from the following verses that tell what the laver signifies. How are we washed today?

Ps. 119:9

John 17:17

Eph. 5:26

The laver was formed from brass mirrors the women of Israel had brought from Egypt. It not only helped the priests see their stains but also allowed them to *wash them away.* It's wonderful that the Bible, which corrects and reproves us, will also cleanse us. "Ye are clean through the word which I have spoken unto you" (John 15:3, KJV), Jesus promises. When we come to the Word, the Spirit literally washes us and changes our minds. It is possible for us to come to the Word, however, and go away without cleansing. We can habitually read and fail to pause for real cleansing.

One evening when our daughter Arla was little, I looked at her hands when she came to dinner and wondered how they could be so grimy. She had washed them —at least the water was on for a few seconds—and she had wiped her hands on the towel. Yet the evidence of the day's play was plainly there.

"Put your hands into the water, Arla," I insisted. Then we scrubbed and allowed soap and running water to cleanse her hands and make them sweet-smelling again.

2. What attitudes are necessary for real cleansing to occur in our lives when we come to the Word?

The priests needed continual cleansing of their hands and feet because they were in constant contact with defilement. The Tabernacle had no floor covering, perhaps to remind us that we always stay in contact with the world. Jesus didn't pray that we would be taken out of the world, but that we would be kept from the evil (John 17:15).

When Jesus prayed, "Sanctify them by the truth; your word is truth" (v. 17), He spoke of a continuing sanctification in daily life.[1]

3. In John 13:10, Jesus told Peter that he needed only to have his feet washed. We continually need to be cleansed from the defilement that we encounter as we go on our way. What will our obeying and believing the Word do for us? Consider 2 Cor. 7:1.

We must keep coming to the laver. "Stop listening to instruction, my son, and you will stray from the words of knowledge" (Prov. 19:27). It is not enough to think we know what the Word says; we must keep listening and let it continually cleanse our thoughts.

4. Perhaps James was thinking of the laver when he compared the Word to a mirror. What does he say is necessary to be changed by it? See James 1:22-25.

How Clean Is Clean?

1. The laver teaches us one thing: To go into the Lord's presence, we must be clean. What would happen to

the priests if they entered without being cleansed? See Exod. 30:20-21.

2. God's Word to us is just as solemn. See Rom. 8:8, 13.

3. We cannot maintain our communion with the Lord unless we're cleansed from all sin. How holy does God expect us to be, according to Eph. 1:4; 5:27?

4. What could God have meant when He said, "Walk before me, and be thou perfect" (Gen. 17:1, KJV)? God uses the word "perfect" much as a man used it when he described a gift his daughter gave him one blistering summer day after he had worked in his garden. He came into the house hot and exhausted. As he sat down to rest, his little girl brought him a glass of ice water. She had been out playing beside him in the garden, and her little fingers, which had dropped the ice into the water, were streaked with dirt. The water was cloudy with some of that dirt. With her other smudged hand, she held up a little piece of potato chip.

"Did I drink that water and eat that chip? Of course. To me it was a perfect gift." That's the kind of perfection God longs for us to offer Him. Our gifts of love may not be perfect in anyone else's eyes, but God knows when our heart's desire is to please Him.

Being perfect means we are so eager to please God

that we're willing for Him to go beneath the surface and show us any hindrances to His being glorified through us. God's Word does this for all who will come with a desire to know the truth. According to Heb. 4:12-13, what will the Word do in your life?

I heard a mother tell about her son's falling and getting a big gash on his leg. She washed the wound and took him to the doctor. The doctor shined his light into the wound, and it revealed that the wound she thought was clean was still full of debris.

We often want to respond like the child who doesn't want the cleansing. "No—it hurts too much! Leave me alone!" But when our desire to glorify God is deeper than all other desires, we're willing for the light of the Holy Spirit to search our hearts.

5. How good are we at knowing our own hearts? See Jer. 17:9.

A recent article in *Science* magazine was titled "Asteroid Scare Provokes Soul-Searching."[2] Astronomers had reported that earth would have a close encounter with an asteroid in 2028. The next day the estimates were revised, however, and the scare was lifted.

On first glance, the title of the article would make us assume that the editors were thinking, "Oh, no—the end of the world is coming! Are we ready to die?" and that the announcement had brought a fear of God. But no—the "soul-searching" referred merely to the question as to whether the astronomers should have announced the close encounter before all the studies had been completed. The report reflected simply on their credibility. Their concern wasn't "Were we doing the most honest thing?" but rather "How did that make us look?"

6. Can you think of evidences that wondering "How does that make me look?" is the deepest soul-searching most people want?

7. An encounter with a holy God reveals truth. What did Isaiah say when he came into God's presence? See Isa. 6:5.

Do you long for the Holy Spirit to give His opinion about your attitudes, deep desires, hidden motives, relationships, and opinions? If so, why is staying in the Word important?

8. We are so good at covering up our motives, even from ourselves, that until God reveals to us what He sees, we excuse our actions. Notice in the following verses that it's God who sees through us completely.

1 Chron. 28:9

Prov. 16:2

Prov. 24:12

1 Thess. 2:4

9. The natural mind values such things as others' opinions or the money to be earned. The mind being cleansed by the Word asks, "Am I pleasing God?" Why do we often not welcome the Spirit's scrutiny of our motives?

10. In all our encounters, decisions, and temptations, we should remember Jacob's words: "Surely the LORD is in this place, and I was not aware of it" (Gen. 28:16). He is in every detail of our lives. Suddenly those private thoughts we had, the secret ambitions, and the conversations behind closed doors are "laid bare before the eyes of him to whom we must give account" (Heb. 4:13).

"Surely you desire truth in the inner parts; you teach me wisdom in the inmost place" (Ps. 51:6). What promise does He give in Ps. 145:18?

11. Don't shrink from the Bible and prayer because they give you a sense of guilt. Remember that the laver, which shows the sin, is also the fountain that will wash it away. Claim the promise of Zech. 13:1.

The Results of Cleansing

What beauty there is in the wholehearted desire to please God, which comes only as we're cleansed by the Word! No wonder the Bible speaks four times about "the beauty of holiness" (1 Chron. 16:29; 2 Chron. 20:21; Pss. 29:2; 96:9, all KJV).

I thought of this beauty when my friend Judy shared a time when the Word cleansed her. Her family frequently had to be with someone who drinks a lot and uses vulgar language. When she told her husband, "I don't like him, and I don't want to be around him," he replied that she was being critical and judgmental. She was hurt by his response, but she prayed, "Is my husband right, Lord?"

She said, "I hold a lot of life's situations up to Ps. 25:4-5: 'Show me your ways, O LORD, teach me your paths; guide me in your truth and teach me, for you are God my Savior.'"

The Lord showed her that this man was really very nice and that she was not to be repelled by what he said or did. The only thing wrong with him was that he didn't know Jesus.

Judy wrote, "My heart softened, and I began to see him through the eyes of Jesus, who dined and ate with sinners and people who seemed to do everything we think hurts the heart of God. In reality, *I* was the one who was hurting His heart by being critical and judgmental."

Is it any wonder that as 1 Pet. 3:1-2 is being fulfilled in her home, her family is coming to Christ? What beauty there is in transparency before God, allowing the Word to judge and humbly accepting the cleansing it provides! When this happens, Jesus' prayer is being answered: we are being sanctified through truth.

1. Notice Paul's confidence in his personal holiness in Phil. 4:9. Why is it necessary to be cleansed by the Word if we are to be a witness to others?

2. A missionary went to India and said he found three kinds of people: those who said about the gospel message he preached, "It's not true"; those who said, "It's not new"; and those who said, "It's not you." The third group was the hardest to win. Why do you think this was true?

"May the words of my mouth be the same as the meditations of my heart," a man prayed in our early morning prayer time at church (see Ps. 19:14). Such purity is attractive both to people and to God.

3. The side benefit that accompanied my efforts to "learn to obey" was the amazing joy that followed obedience. His "words . . . were my joy and my heart's delight" (Jer. 15:16). His words do not become our joy and delight until they become our life, an expression of who we are.

In a recent phone conversation, my son related an employee's irresponsibility and the scripture that had changed his reaction to her. "It's so much fun to do stuff in response to Scripture," he said.

What did Jesus promise to give if we allow His Word to live in us? See John 15:10.

Memorize: The law from your mouth is more precious to me than thousands of pieces of silver and gold *(Ps. 119:72).*

Prayer: *Dear Lord, I praise You as I come to the laver. You've provided a way for me to see if I'm clean, so I can live in Your presence. Give me grace to allow the Holy Spirit to identify any wickedness in my own heart. Cleanse me from secret sins. Let them not have dominion over me. May the words of my mouth and the meditation of my heart be truly pleasing to You. Help me to humble my pride and care only that my life reflects Your truth. In Jesus' name I pray. Amen.*

In God's light we see clearly His will for our lives, and as we reflect His light, others see His glory.

Light—the Symbol of His Presence

Read Exod. 25:31-40; 27:20-21; Lev. 24:1-4.

The lampstand and its utensils contained a talent of pure beaten gold equal to 1,500 ounces and would be worth over $½ million today. Both the center light and its six branches were profusely ornamented. The flower- and fruit-shaped ornaments were formed by hammering the gold and were so arranged that the flames should illuminate the front side of the lampstand. Snuffers and snuff dishes were provided, and only the purest oil could be used.

Fulfilled in Christ

The central lamp reminds us of Christ, who said, "I am the light of the world" (John 9:5). The six branches extending from the sides of the lampstand (Exod. 25:32) may suggest us as believers, for Jesus also said, "You are the light of the world" (Matt. 5:14). Paul urged that we shine as "lights in the world" (Phil. 2:15, KJV).

"I am the light of the world," Jesus said. "Whoever follows me will never walk in darkness, but will have the light of life" (John 8:12).

Directions for Us

The lampstand in the Tabernacle is good news. "The people walking in darkness have seen a great light; on those living in the land of the shadow of death a light has dawned" (Isa. 9:2).

How can we be full of the light of the lampstand? "Your eye is the lamp of your body. When your eyes are good, your whole body also is full of light. But when they are bad, your body also is full of darkness" (Luke 11:34).

If we have a single eye, we focus on one thing. We are looking only to God. In our decision making, we ask the Lord, "What do You want me to do? What will bring You glory? How would You respond in this situation?" If we care only that He is pleased and that He is glorified, then our whole life is full of light.

While studying about the lampstand, I had to make a major business decision. I realized I simply needed to make sure that my eye was single. If I cared only that God was pleased and that He was glorified, then my whole body would be full of light; my understanding would be complete. If I didn't know God's will, it was because either that pleasing Him wasn't my highest desire in this situation or that this was not the particular moment I needed direction.

When we surrender our will to God, we have discernment and wisdom to recognize God's still, small voice. The Light of the World dispels darkness, perplexity, sin, and doubt. "God is light; in him there is no darkness at all" (1 John 1:5). The golden lampstand speaks of the discernment and knowledge the Spirit gives.

One of the greatest privileges of the holy life is the joy of sensing God's leadership, to clearly know He is saying, "Hold it—don't move just yet," and to receive grace to respond to a Spirit-given hesitancy, an inner red light. At other times the Spirit gives a clear inner knowing, a green light that indicates, "This is the time. Say those words; make that purchase."

The golden lampstand was a sevenfold light, seven standing for completeness. When we look to Him, we have all the knowledge we need.

"God . . . made his light shine in our hearts to give us the light of the knowledge of the glory of God in the face of Christ" (2 Cor. 4:6). His Spirit, our inner lampstand, shines within to give us the light of the knowledge of God's glory as we look into the face of Jesus.

Let's consider a few of the lessons taught by the golden lampstand.

Light Gives Revelation

1. The holy place had no windows, so the lampstand was the only source of light in God's sanctuary. This teaches that we are to look only to Him to provide the light that we need.

"Trust in the LORD with all your heart and lean not on your own understanding" (Prov. 3:5). Both of the phrases in this well-known verse are necessary to have our holy place lit with the light of the lampstand. This does not say we can't use our understanding, but we're not to lean on it. What's the difference between the two?

2. Jesus never leaned on His own understanding but always said what the Father prompted Him to say. I think He would have said some pretty good things on His own! Yet if Jesus needed to listen attentively, then certainly we do too. Notice, though, that He refused to say His own words. See John 8:28; 12:49-50.

3. Why do you think Jesus refused to say anything except what the Father gave Him to say?

4. Can we train ourselves to be, as Jesus was, constantly tuned to God's voice? See John 14:10-12.

5. Jesus wants us to have the same relationship He has with the Father. See John 17:21, 23, 26. Just as Jesus did, we can trust the Holy Spirit to direct the details of our lives.

Our son and his wife took a weekend trip. "The only bad thing," he told me, "was that we had to miss our pastor's sermon." In another conversation he shared that their pastor prays several hours a day. I see a connection between those two comments.

Scientists tell us that the amount of light reflected increases dramatically as we move closer to the light source. Likewise, revelation comes to those who are closest to the light through prayer and study of His Word.

Setting Up the Lampstand

1. The lamps were to be set so they would light the space in front of it (Num. 8:2). The light was to shine only in front of the lampstand. Those who walk behind light walk in darkness—they cannot see light. Is it possible to see God's will clearly if we're being disobedient? See 1 John 1:6.

2. Notice our position determines what we see. See Exod. 14:19-20.

3. The lampstand is mentioned in connection with the table (Exod. 40:24-25), also known as the table of the Presence (Num. 4:7). Without His light, we wouldn't know that His bread is available for us to eat and enjoy. Because of His light, we can feed on His Word and absorb His sweetness. "In your light we see light" (Ps. 36:9).

The lampstand is also connected with the burning of the incense on the altar. See Exod. 30:7-8.

How little we understand what to ask when we lean on our own understanding! The Spirit gives us light so we understand how to offer worship and intercession.

4. When God told Moses to set up the lamps, He said they were to keep them burning. See Lev. 24:1-2. This suggests that His people are to be His light shining in the dark world. After noticing this truth, I thought of a friend for whom I had been praying. How would she see my light if I was never with her? I drove to the store where she works. After our greetings, she said, "The Lord sent you. I'm having a bad day—our son's going to court." We receive light not just for ourselves, but to be light for those around us.

Our good works give light to others when we do them for His glory. According to Matt. 5:16, why should we do good deeds?

5. When Jesus said, "I have given them the glory that you gave me" (John 17:22), He probably was saying that we, too, can represent God in the world. We are to carry on the witness that Jesus initiated. See John 20:21.

Using Our Lampstand

The lampstand was to be made of pure gold. What does gold symbolize for us? How are we to provide this channel for the Spirit to flow into our lives continually?

1. What is the New Testament reality for this Old Testament symbol of pure gold? The church at Laodicea was counseled to buy "gold refined in the fire, so you can become rich" (Rev. 3:18). Adam Clarke suggests that this phrase means "faith that shall stand in every trial."[1]

How does 1 Pet. 1:7 compare faith to gold refined by fire?

2. Faith is the coin in the Kingdom life just as gold is the coin in the natural life. What did Jesus say we can purchase through faith? See Matt. 9:2, 22, 29; 17:20.

3. The gold lampstand speaks of our faith as the channel through which the flow of the Holy Spirit, or light, enters our life. When we begin doubting, we're letting in Satan's way of thinking, which brings darkness. Then we can't see clearly. Faith brings light or God's way of seeing. Why must our faith be a moment-by-moment confidence that God is providing the light we need?

4. To maintain this clear, pure light, the priests used two accessories: the tongs and the snuff dishes. With the tongs the priests trimmed the wicks, and with the snuff dishes they carried away the trimmings. The tongs may suggest self-discipline, and the snuff dishes may represent the obedience we must exercise in carrying out His commands.

God wants our daily hindrances removed. For His light and love to shine through us, we must continually exercise self-discipline and obedience. In what areas of your life might a lack of self-discipline hinder you from enjoying fellowship with God or hinder others from seeing His light through you?

5. When we come into God's presence, we see what He disapproves of, what He would remove from us. What happens if we willfully resist? See Rev. 2:5.

6. According to 1 John 1:7, on what does our fellowship with Christ depend?

7. The Israelites were to use the clear oil of pressed olives in the lampstand (Lev. 24:2). People gave the oil as a freewill offering. The freewill offering of Christ brings to us the oil of the Holy Spirit. Gethsemane, the place where Jesus' pressing, bruising, and beating began, means "oil press."

Likewise, our submission to suffering permits others to see God's glory. The Light of the World flows from the surrender of His people. For instance, God's light was evident when

- a father voted not to build a new church, but after the construction was approved by the majority, he worked harder than anyone else on the new building.
- a mother was criticized by others but kept a sweet attitude because she trusted the Lord to defend her.
- a lady endured much sickness without questioning God's goodness.

What evidences of God's grace and glory have you seen through others?

8. Are you facing a difficulty that you will let God use as an "oil press" to bring Him glory?

9. Priests were responsible to keep the lights burning continually (Exod. 27:20; Lev. 24:2). One of the most remarkable truths taught by the lampstand is that we receive the light continually, moment by moment.

Zechariah expands the picture of this lampstand by describing it as being constantly replenished by oil flowing from two olive trees that grew on either side of the lamp. Read 4:1-3, 11-14.

Continually, every moment, the lamp was receiving the oil from the trees. The lamp did not have to produce the oil on its own but simply receive the constant supply from the olive trees. We do not receive enough grace to automatically keep us living victoriously when we believe Him for forgiveness and cleansing. Only through receiving

His grace through moment-by-moment faith do we have perfect light.

How wonderful to have continual direction! God knows we must have that if we're to be His resting-place. Every moment God is providing all the guidance we need.

Memorize: For with you is the fountain of life; in your light we see light *(Ps. 36:9).*

Prayer: *Dear Lord, I praise You for continually filling me with light. As long as I'm trusting You for guidance and Your will is my highest joy, I have all the light I need. Thank You for those times when Your Spirit checks me with an inner hesitancy, teaching me not to lean on my own understanding or to forge ahead. I want to be so responsive to Your Spirit that even when I don't see the way ahead with my senses, I follow where Your Spirit guides my spirit. Thank You for allowing me to live in the Spirit. In Jesus' name I pray. Amen.*

[illegible]

1 [illegible] associations [illegible]

[illegible] emotions

2 " [illegible]

3 [illegible] Relationships

4 [illegible] of faith

5 [illegible] of the first [illegible]

1 Thes 5:[illegible] "Be always joyful —"

Christ waits to spread a feast for you. Your delight in His love will be meat and drink to Him!

Communion at All Times!

READ Exod. 25:23-30; 37:10-16; Lev. 24:5-9.

In the holy place, on the north side, was placed the "table of the Presence" (Num. 4:7). It was made of acacia wood overlaid with pure gold. The table, made of gold-covered acacia wood, held 12 loaves of bread made of fine flour and covered with frankincense. A crown, or molding of gold, encircled the table. Four gold rings were attached to the legs to hold the staves used for carrying the table.

Fulfilled in Christ

Christ is our spiritual food. He said, "I am the living bread that came down from heaven. If anyone eats of this bread, he will live forever. This bread is my flesh, which I will give for the life of the world. . . . My flesh is real food and my blood is real drink. Whoever eats my flesh and drinks my blood remains in me, and I in him" (John 6:51, 55-56).

Now each of us who believes in Christ is a priest and is privileged to eat of that bread, which is Christ.

Directions for Us

"Attend to the One within you." These words filled my mind when I awakened one Sunday morning. With them came a picture of the previous evening. I had been away for several days, and it had been so good to return home and focus on family. Our daughter Arla and her husband,

Kris, had come over, and as we sat around the table eating strawberries and ice cream, I attended to them—eager to absorb their words, to concentrate on what they shared about their days while I was away.

As I thought of our visit, I understood what the Spirit wanted me to do. Absorb His words, be attentive to Him, abide in Him, listen to His words of love.

One day I heard someone pray, "Thank You this day for communion"; and the still small voice said, "When you get up in the morning, don't think, 'I have this and this and this to do,' but think, 'Another day for communion with God!'" As the psalmist discovered, our purpose all the days of our lives is "to gaze upon the beauty of the LORD" (27:4).

How do we commune with the Lord? For Mary it involved sitting at Jesus' feet, loving His words, focusing on Him (Luke 10:39).

My friend Dorothy said she had read someone's suggestion, "Let God love you," and she realized that although she frequently told God she loved Him, she seldom allowed *Him* to love *her.* Communion with God is more than making petitions. It's often not accompanied by words at all. Communion is an attitude of loving contemplation of God, often focusing on taking in His words, and often being accompanied with joy. As it was for Moses, it is "seeing him who is invisible" (Heb. 11:27, KJV). He "persevered because he saw him who is invisible" (v. 27). What strength is found in attending to the One who loves us!

Those whose lives glorify God enjoy communion with Him. To gain understanding of the communion of the Spirit, let's look at God's initial presentation of it in His design of the Tabernacle.

We Satisfy Him!

1. We tend to think of communion with God as simply His gift to us. Amazingly, though, He says our eating with Him is first of all for *His* pleasure! Before the priests

could eat the bread, it was to be offered to God for six days: "Put the bread of the Presence on this table to be before me at all times," God instructed Moses in Exod. 25:30.

In Rev. 3:20, when Christ promises to eat with all those who invite Him into their hearts, whose eating does He mention first?

"For the LORD's portion is his people" (Deut. 32:9). In so many ways God has told us He finds His joy in us.

2. Jesus' death and resurrection beautifully illustrate that the bread is first to be offered to the Father. When Jesus arose, He didn't want Mary to touch Him. "Do not hold on to me," He told her, "for I have not yet returned to the Father" (John 20:17).

Later He let others touch Him, but first He wanted to offer himself to His Father. His sacrificial giving of himself was first of all for God, second for us. Consider the effect that doing all we do first of all for God, second for others, would make in our lives. Would there be more joy? Less burnout? Why?

3. Each loaf was to be covered with frankincense, which the priests burned on the altar while they ate the bread. This symbol spoke of God's pleasure in their communion. The fragrance rose to Him, and He delighted in it.

We can offer no more acceptable service to God than to feed upon Christ and enjoy Him. Martha prepared what she thought Jesus would enjoy eating, but Mary pleased Him more as she sat at His feet. In what does He delight, according to Prov. 15:8, KJV?

4. Jesus said, "I have eagerly desired to eat this Passover with you" (Luke 22:15). Barclay translates this, "I have desired with all my heart to eat this Passover with you."[1] Christ waits to spread a feast for you. Your delight in His love will be satisfying to Him! How should knowing that God enjoys our fellowship affect our devotional lives?

Communion Satisfies Us

A Christian leader was very sick and was not expected to live. Alone with the Lord, He cried, "What should I do, Lord?"

God spoke to his spirit, "Man's chief end is to glorify God, and to enjoy Him forever" (from the Westminster Catechism).

The man, the director of a large Christian organization, realized that he would not have said it that way. He would have said, "The chief end of man is to glorify God, and to serve Him forever." But God is not satisfied simply with service—He wants us to *enjoy* Him.

The Lord allowed the man to recover from his illness, and he now lives with a different purpose—he lives to enjoy his Lord.

1. What would we do differently if we understood that our purpose is to enjoy God rather than to serve Him? Do you think our service would be more effective? If so, why?

2. Jesus is our Living Bread. What was He called in John 6:32-33, 35?

No wonder the disciples prayed, "Lord, give us this bread always" (v. 34, NKJV).

3. In Lev. 24:5-9 God instructed the Israelites to bake 12 loaves—a loaf for each tribe. Each loaf was to be made of two-tenths of an ephah (about four quarts) of flour, so as to provide enough food for a man and his neighbor. God knows the exact loaf each needs, so we can trust Him to provide exactly what we need ourselves as well as what we need to give to others in family devotions, Bible study, Sunday School class, or any other time we give out the Word.

Do you recall a time when God provided the exact word that fed your spirit?

"The taste of it [manna] was like wafers made with honey" (Exod. 16:31, KJV). Jewish authorities tell us, "It tasted to every man as he pleased." In other words, it suited every palate, whether young or old. How remarkable, considering there were many thousands of people to satisfy!

This, then, is the food on which we can feed and be completely satisfied. It is only when we stray from the Father's table that we cry, "How many of my father's hired men have food to spare, and here I am starving to death!" (Luke 15:17).

4. Feeding upon Christ is a joy we can experience anywhere. Bread was always to be bread on the table in the Tabernacle. Even when the Israelites were traveling, bread was to remain on the table. See Num. 4:1-7. What are ways you can find nourishment throughout your day?

5. We are invited to feed upon Him in our spirits even when we feel unworthy. Although no priest with a defect was permitted to serve at the altar of incense, he was permitted to eat the bread in the holy place. See Lev. 21:21-23. Consider how this speaks to us of Christ's love. Even though we may be too spiritually cold to minister to others, Christ desires to feed and cherish us. We can come and feed on Him until we gain strength to serve. How can this encourage you on those days Satan tells you that you're unworthy to enjoy Christ's fellowship?

When I was a little girl, my grandfather lived with us. On Sunday evenings my father would often go to Grandpa's room just to be with him. Grandpa was hard of hearing, so communication was difficult. Most of the time they seemed to simply share each other's presence.

Those times of communion satisfied them for two reasons. Grandpa deeply loved my father, and my father was showing his joy in Grandpa by being with him. In a similar way, our communion with our Heavenly Father is satisfying.

Communion Gives Life!

To begin to understand how to eat and drink at the spiritual Communion table, we need to compare two scriptures. Read Mark 14:22-25 and John 6:32-35, 53-58. We'll discuss the bread first and then the wine.

1. When Jesus established the first Communion under the new covenant, how did He define the bread? See Mark 14:22 and John 6:32-35.

2. What does John 1:14 say became Jesus' flesh?

3. We commune with Him, then, through the Word. His life is in the Word, so the Word is living (Heb. 4:12). When we take in His Word and assimilate the Living Word by obedience, we, too, have life. This truth is taught all through Scripture. For instance, see Deut. 32:47 and Neh. 9:29.

4. The invitation to commune with Him is an invitation to feed on His Word and to let it become our lives. According to the *Jewish New Testament Commentary,* "To eat the flesh is to absorb His entire way of being and living."[2] We read, think, and meditate on the Word with a longing to believe it, act on it, and live it out until it becomes the expression of who we are. We are then living out Christ's life, and He is being formed in us.

"Let the word of Christ dwell in you richly" (Col. 3:16). The results of our communion will be the answer to Paul's prayer. See Gal. 4:19.

5. What is the condition of those who do not feed on Him, according to John 6:53? Why is this true? Can you think of evidences of this in society? (To the Hebrews, to have life meant to have vitality, joy, a sense of fulfillment and satisfaction—all that made life worthwhile.)

6. "We are what we eat," we say of physical food. Our spiritual body is the same. It's so easy to absorb the spirit of the world. What are ways we do that?

7. Cups filled with wine rested next to the bread. When Jesus established the first Communion under the new covenant, how did He define wine? See Mark 14:23-25.

8. Reread John 6:53-57, and write at least three truths about His blood (the wine of the new covenant).

9. The Blood speaks of Jesus' self-sacrifice and passionate desire to obey His Father. To drink His blood, then, is to absorb His self-sacrificing Spirit. It is not enough to take in the Word (eat His flesh). If obeying those words is an irksome duty that we do only to escape punishment, there's no joy in it.

My relationship with God changed when I began to see the Word not as something to be dutifully read and learned, but as truth to be lived because I love God and want to please Him. Then to my amazement, that obedience became the joy in my life!

What are reasons, other than love, some might attempt to obey the Word?

10. When we remember that God is seeking a loving relationship, we understand why He gives life to those who keep His commands with love. What does Jesus say in John 14:24 is necessary to do to keep His commands?

11. Why do you think it is impossible to love Jesus without obeying Him?

12. One recent Christmas season I was meditating on a phrase from Col. 3:4, "Christ, who is your life." Perhaps because it was party time and I was remembering that we speak of people who are "the life of the party," I said with reverent, exuberant joy, "Christ, You are 'the life of my party.'" The inner joy I have through communion with Him is life—abundant life!

"The life of the flesh is in the blood." Rewrite these words from Lev. 17:11 (KJV), using the descriptions discussed in this section. ("Life" means "joy"; "the flesh" means "the Word"; "the blood" speaks of willing surrender.)

13. Our communion with God will have no life if our efforts for His presence are not accompanied by a loving surrender to His will. It's not enough to grudgingly obey the commands of God as a list of rules. Life is in doing what God says because we love Him and because our joy is in pleasing Him.

What joy, what contentment we have when all we do has this underlying message to our loving Lord: "I'm doing this because I love You!" All of life then becomes holy and lived in the holy place.

Again, we see a loving God not seeking for a people who follow laws, but seeking for a people who have one desire—to please Him.

Why would communion with God be impossible without a passion to please Him?

14. Jewish writers tell us that when Jesus instituted the Communion, He was referring to a satisfying portion of bread and a refreshing drink—not the morsel of bread and sip of wine offered at Communion services today. The Lord's Supper was a real meal, a time of building relationship, not simply a symbolic ritual.[3]

How satisfying and refreshing to feed on truth and express it by showing Him our love! When we learn to drink of this "wine," we will say to the Master of the Feast, "You have saved the best till now" (John 2:10).

What blessed, sweet communion!

Memorize: Just as the living Father sent me and I live because of the Father, so the one who feeds on me will live because of me *(John 6:57).*

Prayer: *Dear Lord, I'm learning the importance of coming to my time alone with You as though I'm coming to a lover—longing for Your nearness, wanting to enjoy Your fellowship, and seeking to commune with You. Even if my time is shorter than I like, help me to focus on loving You, expecting to hear You speak through Your Word. In Jesus' name I pray. Amen.*

When a hunger for God to be glorified permeates our lives, all we ask can be expressed as a longing for Him to receive glory. How privileged we are to have access to God in prayer!

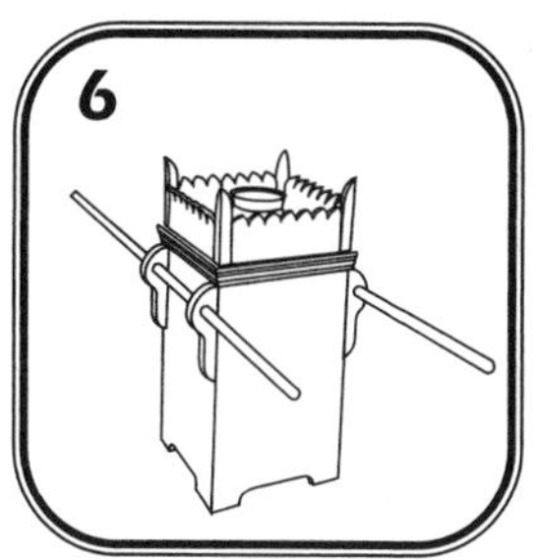

Kneeling at the Golden Altar of Incense

READ Exod. 30:1-10; 37:25-28.

The altar of incense, made of acacia wood and covered with gold, was a place of perpetually burning incense. It was the third article of furniture in the sanctuary, and it stood in the holy place next to the curtain between the holy place and the holy of holies. Incense was made of precious spices according to divine directions and offered on the altar perpetually, night and morning.

"Put the altar in front of the curtain that is before the ark . . . where I will meet with you" (Exod. 30:6).

Fulfilled in Christ

Christ not only bled for us on the Cross but also pleads for us before the heavenly throne. The perpetually burning fire is suggestive of Christ's continual intercession for us at the right hand of God. "He is able to save completely those who come to God through him, because he always lives to intercede for them" (Heb. 7:25).

Directions for Us

When God is free to call us His dwelling place, we frequently find ourselves drawn to prayer. "My house will be called a house of prayer," Jesus said in Mark 11:17. We see a lonely teen, know of a frustrated mother, or hear of a family in crisis; and, if the Holy Spirit is at home within us, we often respond with prayer and other assistance.

The sweet breath of burning spices speaks of the sweet breath of prayer. God receives our prayers as fragrant sacrifices. He promises that there at the golden altar, "I will meet with you" (Exod. 30:6).

Although the golden altar was in the holy place, it "belonged to the inner sanctuary" (1 Kings 6:22). In fact, the writer to the Hebrews wrote that the most holy place "had the golden altar of incense" (9:4). We understand that the golden altar of incense is the place of transition into the holy of holies, because it's through prayer and worship that we are free to enter into His presence.

In Deut. 10:8 the priests were given three duties: to carry the ark of the covenant, to minister to the Lord, and to pronounce blessings in His name. God could have used the word "pray," but instead He uses the richer phrase "pronounce blessings." It's as though we ask that those we pray for be blessed, and it is done.

"I give your priesthood to you as a gift" (Num. 18:7, NKJV). We as believers have also received that gift. Peter refers to believers as "a holy priesthood" (1 Pet. 2:5). What a precious gift God has given us!

The Fragrant Incense

When the priests burned the incense upon the golden altar, the fragrance filled the whole Tabernacle. The sense of smell is perhaps the most delicate, the finest of all our senses, and it is with this that God describes how He receives our prayers.

1. When we pray, our prayers are lovingly saved as in-

cense to be used in worship in heaven. How does Jesus state this in Rev. 5:8; 8:3-4?

2. I love the fragrance of a bouquet of lilacs or the scent of a burning vanilla candle. What represents the most delightful fragrance to you? God chose the sweet aroma of burning spices to speak of our prayer and praise. When we lift the desires and love of our hearts to God, He receives them as though they are a precious fragrance. It is as though He refreshes himself with our worship.

May our prayers always be a delightful fragrance to Him. See David's prayer in Ps. 141:2.

The fire on the altar was to be always burning, and the sweet fragrance of the incense continually rising. We cannot say words all the time as we carry on with the rest of life, but the incense can rise. The reverence and devotion of our hearts can continually rise to God when we learn to dwell in Him with our spirits.

A. B. Simpson, speaking of this concept, said that when he worked in his garden, he could continually enjoy smelling the roses; yet they did not keep him from his gardening. We, too, can be busy all the time and yet be sending a sweet fragrance to God and enjoying His presence. Simpson said, "It is like working in a perfumed room, every sense exhilarated."[1]

Acknowledge the Holy Spirit within you as you go through your day. Delight in His presence. He gives us His life through the Word, so take a phrase of Scripture with you to enjoy.

3. What phrase in Heb. 11:27 gives us the key to Moses' communion with God? Notice that this was the source of his strength.

4. What kind of incense are we to offer? Begin with the spirit of praise and thanksgiving. The priests never came to offer incense without offering thanks. Notice in Heb. 13:15 that we, too, are called to continually bring a spirit of praise.

"Let the high praises of God be in their mouth" (Ps. 149:6, KJV). Comments on this verse in Spurgeon's *Treasury of David* give a new perspective on why the Lord so frequently calls us to praise Him. Why does God call our praises "high"?

"Now the Lord, who is of the most perfect understanding, and deepest skill and knowledge, declares himself to take infinite delight in His people's praises. It is His solace and pleasure to be attended with them, either in earth or in heaven, by men or angels; and His soul is ravished with the thoughts and contemplation of them."[2]

Our praises give solace and pleasure to God. Selah! (Pause and think on that.)

5. We're to cultivate the habit of praising God, not just to obey a command or to gain victory over the enemy, but out of a desire to delight Him. See Ps. 69:30.

6. One of our greatest surprises in heaven may be to learn how precious our prayers are to God. The Lord wants fellowship with His children, and He offers His fellowship to us. See Exod. 30:6; Deut. 4:7; and Prov. 15:8.

7. We tend to think God is looking for workers, but He's looking for *worshipers.* See John 4:23-24.

We praise God, not merely because He enjoys our thanksgiving and praise, but, as C. S. Lewis observes, our understanding and enjoyment are incomplete without praise. It is in the process of being worshiped that God communicates His presence to us.[3]

8. God warned against using any incense other than what He chose. Great caution was taken that the incense should be properly composed, of the right materials, in the right proportion.

We are to take equal care with our incense. To approach God with unworthy thoughts, to ask Him for selfish advantages, is to "pray amiss" or to approach Him with "strange incense."

Nor are we to use expressions that are mere clichés, which we hardly have to think to say. What we should aim for is to reflect "the mind of Christ" (1 Cor. 2:16).

Ruth and several others meet on Friday nights at their church for a two-hour prayer vigil. She told me, "We come to listen to what to ask and then pray that back to Him." Listening is a very important part of our praying.

We are foolish to rush into God's presence and ask the first thing that comes into our minds. When we first come, we should be silent and look to Him to send His Spirit to teach us how to pray.

God wants us to listen for His voice rather than get caught up in our own words. Don't we choose our words more carefully if we're listening closely to someone?

"Do not be quick with your mouth, do not be hasty in your heart to utter anything before God" (Eccles. 5:2). Why do you think we're to consider carefully what we say to God?

One lady said, "One day during prayer, the Lord said, 'Today I want you only to praise Me for those on your prayer list. Don't ask for anything.' He still requests that occasionally." Be sensitive to the possibility that at times the Spirit may desire that of you too.

9. Praying scripture surely is offering a proper incense. What does Paul tell us to take to prayer in Eph. 6:17-18?

One night during prayer, I wrote a prayer for my son Gregg and his wife, Sarah. At the end of the prayer I wrote, "I am satisfied if You are glorified," something I often tell the Lord.

I thought of signing Jesus' name to my prayer, and, as I did, it seemed to be a very powerful, awesome thing to do. I realized I had truly prayed in His name, and He was pleased to have His name at the bottom of that prayer.

The next morning, words of the song "God Will Take Care of You" came to me like this: "I will take care of them / Through ev'ry day, o'er all the way"; and I knew it was the Lord's word to me in answer to the first prayer I prayed with His name signed to it.

Moments later, Gregg called to tell that during the night a tornado had narrowly missed his office. This was the first of many times since the night I wrote that prayer that I've recognized God has fulfilled His promise to take care of them.

10. For repeated invitations to pray in His name, see John 14:13-14; 15:16; 16:23-24, 26.

11. Write a prayer here or in your personal prayer journal that you know to be one He is pleased for you to bring to the golden altar. Sign Jesus' name.

12. Fire was necessary for the incense to burn. This fire represents the fire of the Spirit, which helps us to see a need and prompts us to ask what He wants to give. When He carries our prayers to the Father, it is as though we're asking for what was in God's heart. When we sense the Spirit is praying through us, we know He will give what He himself has already asked.

See the call to pray in the Spirit in Eph. 6:18 and Jude 20.

The Altar's Design

The golden altar was crowned with a rim of gold around the top. We have a royal priesthood, and when we come to the golden altar of incense, we are given the royal privilege of intercession. When we call someone's name in prayer, God prepares that person's heart to receive His grace.

1. What authority do we have through prayer? See John 15:7; 16:23.

2. As royalty, we are not to plead with uncertainty, but with authority and assurance of victory. Notice the authority Jesus had in His praying in Luke 22:32.

3. God "calls things that are not as though they were" (Rom. 4:17). At times God spoke to Moses and Joshua in the present perfect tense, as when He said, "I have given them into your hand" (Josh. 10:8). God gives us such authority in prayer that, through faith, we can be as certain of

victory as though the situation were already past. Notice the phrases in the following verses that gave assurance of victory before the battle.

Deut. 2:24

Josh. 6:2

Josh. 8:1

4. Each of the four corners of the altar held horns that may represent the four points of the compass and the different camps of Israel. The prayers of Jesus reach all His people. None of us is outside His prayers. This moment His prayers are saying, "Father, give him or her victory." As we praise and trust Him for it, victory is ours.

Our prayers, too, must be very inclusive. It's easy to pray for only a few of those nearest to us, but to be like Christ we must be open to loving through prayer all those He brings to our minds, in all parts of the world. We'll find that we have many rewards in heaven if our prayer lives reach out in all directions.

In Ps. 2:8, God promises, "Ask of me, and I will make the nations your inheritance, the ends of the earth your possession." We seldom ask for the end of our blocks, much less the ends of the earth.

Who should we include in our praying? Consider 1 Tim. 2:1-2.

5. God asked that they put rings on the golden altar. They could carry it wherever they went. Aren't we grateful that fragrant incense can arise from our spirits to God

wherever we are? Paul said, "I want men everywhere to lift up holy hands in prayer" (1 Tim. 2:8).

God never intended for us to pray in the morning and then leave the golden altar behind as we go to work, to the mall, on a picnic. He has so made our spirits that He can teach us to be in communion with Him at any time. What are practical ways we can make this golden altar a part of our daily lives?

6. "My house will be a house of prayer" (Luke 19:46). "And we are his house" (Heb. 3:6). The more we learn to respond to the Holy Spirit, the more we find He often will give us a spirit of prayer. If the Holy Spirit said, "I want you to be My house of prayer," how should we change in response? What do you think He intends for our lives to look like as His house of prayer?

The altar was the highest object in the holy place. God views prayer and worship as the most exalted service we can offer Him. Our prayers for others make us exceedingly precious to Him.

Prayer is the greatest of all ministries, the best thing we can do for God. A. B. Simpson said, "Even when we think our prayers have had no effect, they have been more effective than all other efforts."

7. If only we could have as high a view of prayer as God does, how much more we would value our prayer time! Jesus, who has perfect understanding of the merits of prayer, lives to make intercession. When our lives most reflect His, we will also live to make intercession. What would you say you live to do?

8. What would your family say you live to do?

9. David longed passionately to provide a resting-place for God. Notice the difference between his intense longing and our frequent complacency toward prayer. See Ps. 132:4-5.

Adrian Rogers on his radio program told that Yonggi Cho, the pastor of the largest church in the world, said he must have his prayer time. One day Rev. Cho told his secretary, "I'm going to prayer, and I don't want anyone to interrupt me—no one, unless it's the Lord Jesus."

That day the president of Korea came to see him. The secretary apologized that she could not disturb the minister.

Later the president's wife told Rev. Cho, "You should fire that secretary. My husband is the president of Korea, and your secretary wouldn't let him speak to you."

"I was speaking with the President of the universe," replied Rev. Cho.

Sometimes it may be pleasing to God for us to respond to God-sent interruptions, but we can trust Him to give us the discernment needed when our desire is to be His house of prayer.

Memorize: I will do whatever you ask in my name, so that the Son may bring glory to the Father. You may ask me for anything in my name, and I will do it *(John 14:13-14).*

Prayer: *Dear Lord, I love knowing You meet with me and receive my incense with joy. How I delight in thinking of being Your 'house of prayer'! Help me to be responsive to the Spirit of prayer. I want my life to be poured-out praise, a never-ending expression of gratitude, worship, and adoration. I praise You for the joy I have as I draw near You through faith. In Jesus' name. Amen.*

When our view of the blood of Jesus is as high as God's is, we'll know He can remove every trace of sin from our lives.

Have You Seen the Lamb?

READ Exod. 25:17-22; 37:6-9.

On the ark of the covenant rested a slab of gold called the "gold atonement cover," or "mercy seat." It was stained by the blood of an animal brought into the holy of holies once a year by the high priest. God promised to meet His people here. "There, above the cover between the two cherubim that are over the ark of the Testimony, I will meet with you and give you all my commands" (Exod. 25:22).

The law the Israelites had broken was inside the ark of the covenant. God would be looking at that broken law, but when the blood was applied, their sins were covered. No wonder it was called the "mercy seat"!

Gold cherubim looked down upon the atonement cover. Perhaps they represent the awe the heavenly beings have for this holiest place, the blood-sprinkled mercy seat. "Even angels long to look into these things" (1 Pet. 1:12).

Fulfilled in Christ

The good news is that Jesus became our Lamb, and His blood covers our sin. The blood sprinkled by the high priest pointed to His shed blood. "How much more, then, will the blood of Christ, who through the eternal Spirit offered himself unblemished to God, cleanse our consciences from acts that lead to death, so that we may serve the living God!" (Heb. 9:14).

Christ, the One whose blood covers our sins, is the meeting place between God and the sinner.

Fulfilled in Us

Amy's parents were Buddhists, and because she was a frail child, they dedicated her to two gods. When she was in her 20s, Amy became a Christian. One night as she lay in bed, she felt she was being choked. The next morning she had bruises on her arms and black eyes as though she had been pinched repeatedly. She told a Christian friend about it, and her friend replied, "The next time this happens, say 'In the name of Jesus,' plead the Blood, and praise the Lord." (To plead the Blood is to ask for everything Jesus' blood has provided for that person or that situation.)

A month later Amy felt as if a great evil power had swept over her. She said, "I remembered my friend's advice and called out 'In the name and blood of Jesus!' Immediately the evil power disappeared!"

The blood of Jesus holds great mystery. The love and power that it represents deserve our sincere attention.

In the Book of Revelation, a future scene was enacted in John's spirit. He saw "a mighty angel proclaiming in a loud voice, 'Who is worthy to break the seals and open the scroll?' But no one in heaven or on earth or under the earth could open the scroll or even look inside it. I wept and wept because no one was found who was worthy to open the scroll or look inside" (5:2-4).

Why did John weep? John understood that the scroll was the "Book of redemption."[1] If no one could open that book, then all hope of our redemption was gone.

Then someone gave him the good news that represents the pivotal point of all eternity: a Lamb was slain! All our tears are dried when we see the Lamb.

Once a year on Yom Kippur, the Day of Atonement, the high priest entered the holiest place in the Tabernacle, carrying the names of the people on his breastplate to make reconciliation for their sins. He would go through the veil that separated the holy place from the most holy place and would sprinkle the blood of animals on the golden cover of the ark of the covenant. See Lev. 16:2, 15-16.

God Wants Us Near Him!

The price we will pay for something tells how much we value it. A major television network recently announced with great celebration that they had purchased the rights to air next year's football games for $500 million. I was struck by the announcer's obvious joy when speaking of this purchase, which would bring new programming and up to 50 percent of the homes in Kansas City watching this programming on their channel. He wasn't saying he was happy the network got a bargain, but rather that he was happy the network could pay what it took to get what they wanted.

Do you know what your communion cost God? Do you know how badly He wanted it?

God knew the price He must pay to secure the fellowship of sinful humanity, but His heart so longed for us to be able to draw near Him at any time that, amazingly, He willingly paid the price. Surely that must be the meaning of Isa. 53:10: "Yet it pleased the LORD to bruise him" (KJV). What else could these words mean? They make sense only when we understand that they express God's intense longing to have us near Him. Our nearness is so precious to Him that He willingly paid the ultimate price for it.

1. What was the price of our redemption? See Acts 20:28 and 1 John 4:9-10.

2. Jesus is highly valued in heaven because He was the Lamb who made us to be kings and priests. He is worshiped and praised for that! What does Rev. 5:6-10 say about the value God places upon our fellowship with Him?

3. God's heart so longs for us to draw near Him that He freely gave His Son's blood to purchase our nearness. We honor the Blood and His love by confidently entering the holiest with great boldness. How does He invite us to come in Heb. 4:16?

4. Write three insights you gain about our drawing near God from Heb. 10:19-23.

One early morning as I drove to a meeting, I realized I had failed to have personal devotions. At one time I would have felt unworthy of drawing near to God. But I remembered the Blood and realized that even three hours of devotions wouldn't earn me a place in His holy presence. Because of Jesus' shed blood, with boldness I drew near and enjoyed communion with Him as I drove.

5. What should be our response to a God who loves us so much that He was pleased to have His Son shed His blood to draw us near Him?

The mercy seat was the exact size of the ark of the covenant that it covered, telling us that God's mercies always fit our needs exactly.

The Blood Provides Forgiveness of Sins

I spoke at a retreat that had the theme "Clean Hands, Pure Heart." In one session a lady turned to me during the song service and handed me a piece of paper on which she had written, "My hands are dirty. The blood of my child is on my hands. I need to wash my hands so I can have a pure heart and can lift my hands without shame, honoring God."

"I had an abortion when I was 19, and I can't feel forgiven," she whispered. Pain and sorrow filled her eyes.

At the close of the service, she prayed at the altar. The next morning she told the women of her guilt from her abortion. Then she added, "Yesterday when I knelt at the altar, Jesus was there. He reached out His hands to me, and I saw that the blood of my child was on His hands. My hands were clean!"

That's exactly what Jesus' blood does for us. "Atonement" means to cover or to cancel. How often we spend moments, days, even years feeling guilty for a past wrong. We have only to look to Jesus' blood and accept His forgiveness. God remembers our sins no more (Heb. 8:12; 10:17). Our hands are as clean as though we had never sinned.

1. A great Tabernacle truth is in the songs that speak of being "covered by the Blood" and "constantly abiding, under the atoning Blood." The animal's blood covered the broken Law, just as Jesus' blood covers our sins. What phrases speak of this in Ps. 32:1-2 and Rom. 4:7-8?

If we have come to Christ and have trusted that His blood atones for our sins, God sees the Blood on the atonement cover, and our sins are covered.

Under the old covenant, the priests had to offer animal sacrifices; but according to Hebrews, the sacrifices did not clear their consciences. Instead, their animal sacrifices pointed to the One who would come and remove both our sin and our guilt.

2. Contrast the inefficiency of the Law with the efficiency of the new covenant. Look at Heb. 9:9, 14.

3. Romans 3:25-26 states that God presented Jesus as our atonement. According to these verses, to whom does this apply?

"Boldness" is not necessarily a conscious feeling of confidence, but the objective assurance that our access is a God-given right. A pastor used to quote these anonymous lines about Martin Luther:

Someone once asked Luther,
"Do you feel you've been forgiven?"
He answered, "No, but I'm as sure
As there's a God in heaven.
For feelings come and feelings go,
And feelings are deceiving.
My warrant is the Word of God—
Naught else is worth believing."

The Blood Provides Cleansing of Sin

1. God dwells in a holy place. To dwell with Him, we, too, must be holy. What does Ps. 24:3-4 say is required?

2. We need Jesus' blood to do more than provide forgiveness of sins. Those who enter His presence must have not only clean hands but also pure hearts. Hands refer to our deeds, but our hearts refer to something deeper—our inner desires and motives. Because Adam sinned, we're born with an unholy or sinful nature. See Rom. 5:12.

3. Just as we are certain that a young copperhead will be poisonous, we can be sure that every child will possess a nature that is an enemy to God. What phrases in Ps. 51:5; 58:3-4 describe humanity's corrupt nature?

4. Why did Jesus come, according to 1 John 3:8?

5. No Greek word meaning "suppression" is ever used to describe what God wants to do with inbred sin. What words are used in the following passages?

1 John 3:8-9

Rom. 6:6

Eph. 4:22

6. The blood of Christ has power to purge, cleanse, thoroughly whiten, completely destroy the works of the devil. For the sinner, God uses words such as "justify" and

"forgive." But when He speaks to Christians concerning this deeper work, He uses words that emphasize the destruction of this "body of sin."

What good news it is to know that Jesus' blood not only forgives our sins but also cleanses us from the sin nature! We don't ask to be forgiven for the sin nature we inherited from Adam—we ask to be *cleansed* of it.

Note in the following verses the connection between sin's total destruction and Jesus' sacrifice:

Heb. 9:26

Heb. 10:10

Heb. 10:14

1 John 1:7

"Greater is he that is in you, than he that is in the world" (1 John 4:4, KJV).

Jesus' death provided for inner cleansing. "On that day a fountain will be opened to the house of David and the inhabitants of Jerusalem, to cleanse them from sin and impurity" (Zech. 13:1).

How do you plunge into that cleansing fountain?

a. Acknowledge that His blood has provided cleansing.

b. Trust that His blood now cleanses you.

Trust and Obey—Day of Atonement Rules

1. When God gave the Day of Atonement instructions in Lev. 23:26-32, He was telling us, "To stand in My presence, you must come exactly as I require." To draw near God, we, too, must follow the instructions for the annual Day of Atonement.

What two thoughts are repeated in this passage?

2. *Do no work.* These words speak to us today of simply having faith in Jesus' shed blood. What happened if the Israelites disobeyed this command? See Lev. 23:30.

3. To us, this says we will have no spiritual life when we put faith in our own efforts. Our faith must be only in Jesus' shed blood. What works do people do to try to make themselves holy?

4. How do our works say to God that we consider Jesus' blood to be insufficient?

The last thing to overcome before we are made holy by Jesus' blood is unbelief. A bold confidence in the Blood—not in our efforts, regardless of how wonderful they may be—gives us access into His presence.

5. *Deny yourself.* What are the results of not denying self? See Lev. 23:29.

6. When we deny self, whose will do we obey—ours or God's?

7. Denying self, in a word, is obedience. Although we cannot earn His favor with our good works, we dare not think His blood covers us if we willfully disobey Him. This law of the Day of Atonement teaches us we cannot disobey His law (do what we want rather than what He asks) and then dwell in His presence.

Notice how frequently God stated this qualification of the Day of Atonement. See Lev. 16:29, 31; 23:26-32.

8. Does His blood cover presumptuous sin—a sin that says, "I know what You want, God, but I will do what I want anyway"? For insight read Rom. 6:12-14 and Heb. 9:7.

9. Can grace be used as a cover for unconfessed, deliberate sin? Can we continue sinning and still be covered by the Blood? What does Heb. 10:26-31 say about sins committed after we learn God's requirements?

Even in the Old Testament, the sacrifices were not for the people's willful sins—those sins they knew God forbade, but they committed anyway. Mercy was given, though, if they confessed and turned from their sin. They received forgiveness through faith (do no work) and obedience (deny yourself).

Memorize: We have confidence to enter the Most Holy Place by the blood of Jesus *(Heb. 10:19).*

Prayer: *Dear Lord Jesus, how little I've regarded the Blood, the Blood that gives me access into the most holy place. I thank You that Your blood cleanses me from all sin. When I see You hanging on the cruel Cross, the Blood pouring from Your wounded side, I am enabled to go into Your presence. You are the perfect Lamb of God, who takes away the sin of the world.*

Thank You, Lord, for the love that caused Your blood to be shed for me. I acknowledge that Your blood provides cleansing for my sinful nature, and I trust that Your blood now cleanses me. I give You praise in Your holy name. Amen.

A holy life is not characterized by following a list of dos and don'ts, but by an inner desire to please a holy God. The holy of holies is within!

Christ in Us, the Hope of Glory

Read Exod. 25:10-22; 37:1-5.

The ark of the covenant was a chest made of acacia wood overlaid completely within and without with pure gold. It had a band of gold around its top and a golden ring on each of its four corners. The rings held two poles of gold-covered acacia wood so the ark could be carried.

At first the ark held only the Ten Commandments. Later additions were a golden pot of manna (Exod. 16:33-36) and the budding rod of Aaron (Num. 17:8-10). The ark led the Israelites' procession in all their travels. When they were camping, it rested in the holy of holies.

Fulfilled in Christ

The acacia wood speaks of the humanity of Christ and the gold of His divinity. The unbroken tables within the ark remind us of Christ's perfect obedience. "I desire to do your will, O my God; your law is within my heart" (Ps. 40:8).

Fulfilled in Us

The ark of the covenant was the central piece, the heart of the Tabernacle. The ark speaks beautifully of Christ's presence resting in us and tells us that we are carriers of His presence. We can think of the ark as Christ in us, His Spirit being at home within our spirits.

When the Israelites were traveling and the ark was going ahead of them, they were to maintain a distance behind it to show reverence. Likewise, we should have a sense of awe, reverence, and the realization of His glory within. The indwelling Christ should never become a trivial matter with us.

When we're with a non-Christian, we bring the presence of Christ to that person. Christ's presence within us is a reality and often makes more of a difference than we realize. A friend related that when the nurses spoke of her Christian mother's hospital room, they would say, "Something's different about that room." A nurse told me that patients have asked her, for no reason that she can determine, "You're a Christian, aren't you?" She carries Christ's presence with her.

Carrying the ark was the priests' first role mentioned in Deut. 10:8. "The LORD set apart the tribe of Levi to carry the ark of the covenant of the LORD." We as His priests are now the carriers of His presence. He "has made us to be a kingdom and priests to serve his God and Father" (Rev. 1:6).

Let's consider some of the awesome benefits of being a carrier of His presence.

The Joy of His Presence!

To carry His presence is to be in fellowship with a happy God. "God's glory consists much in the fact that he is happy beyond our wildest imagination," writes John Piper in *The Pleasures of God.*[1] So to live with His presence within us is to have great joy.

1. How do the following glimpses of heaven tell us that great joy exists where God is?

Job 38:4, 7

Matt. 25:21, 23

Luke 15:7, 10

Acts 2:28

2. What does Jesus want to give us, according to John 15:11; 17:13?

3. "The LORD your God has arrived to live among you. He is a mighty savior. He will rejoice over you with great gladness. With his love, he will calm all your fears. He will exult over you by singing a happy song" (Zeph. 3:17, NLT). Think of what the promise of having His joy within us means! Which of these phrases mean the most to you?

4. "Our 'God is a consuming fire'" (Heb. 12:29), and to welcome His presence is to welcome not only His joy but also His cleansing, purifying fire. We love to have His joy, but to continually live with Him is to live with an awareness of when our wrong attitudes and actions displease Him. He lives in a holy place. Consider why the continual surrender and being cleansed by the Word are essentials to maintaining His joy.

5. What promise of joy does God give concerning His resting-place in Ps. 132:8-9? Notice that it is repeated in verses 14-16.

6. When David brought the ark of the covenant back to Jerusalem, he appointed worship leaders. What were they to do regularly before the ark? See 1 Chron. 16:4-6.

His presence still dwells in the midst of praise. As our spirits praise God, He is present, and we sense His joy. "In thy presence is fulness of joy," exclaimed the psalmist (16:11, KJV).

His Presence Gives Guidance

Imagine being an Israelite and always, every day, at each step of the journey knowing exactly which way to go. The Israelites never had to say, "I wonder where God wants me to go today." Rather, "the ark of the covenant of the LORD went before them . . . to find them a place to rest" (Num. 10:33).

Even more wonderful is having the reality of what the ark symbolized—the presence of Christ within. With Him we have the possibility of enjoying constant communion and guidance.

1. God wants us to know that His presence will be with us continually. Poles were to be inserted into the rings for carrying the ark of the covenant. In all the other pieces of furniture the poles could be removed, but they were never to be removed from the ark. What promises in the following references encourage you to continually be confident of His presence?

Deut. 31:6, 8

Ps. 41:12

Matt. 28:20

Heb. 13:5

2. This glorious ark of the covenant led the people and constantly promised guidance and victory. When the Israelites needed to know which way to go, they followed the ark of the covenant. Wherever they went, it went before them. For example, see Josh. 3:1-4, 11.

3. God still goes before us, finding us a place to rest. When the Spirit checks us—"Don't go there"; "Don't say that"—He is leading us to the place of rest He's found. He goes ahead, and if enemies are there, He scatters them.

Notice in Num. 14:41-45 the defeat that followed when the Israelites did not wait for the ark.

4. The presence of Christ within will lead all those who follow Him. Consider Gal. 5:25.

How prone we are to forget to follow the ark (the presence of Christ within), proceeding as though we can somehow make it on our own! For instance, we look at someone's successful ministry and think that patterning our actions after theirs will bring success. If other armies had known of the Israelites' success, they might have inquired, "Exactly what time of the day did you cross?" "How far did the leaders step into the Jordan?" On and on, as though the secret lay in the detail of the plans. The Israelites' secret was that they followed the ark.

5. Our "successes" are empty when we accomplish them in our own strength. Restate Ps. 127:1 in your own words, applying it to a situation in your own life.

The house (of Ps. 127:1) may be built, the church pews filled, the people entertained, the Bible study led; but unless God does the work, nothing is really done. Often we are blinded because we appear to have built something. We have convinced someone of his or her error, have entertained people, or have seen our crowd double; but we discover that no one actually had a supernatural parting of the waters in his or her life.

6. In what types of situations are you tempted not to look to Christ's presence within you?

"I would obey if I only knew what He wants me to do," we sometimes respond. But we must respond in faith. Not only will we do what He wants us to do, but also we'll trust that He'll lead us. We trust that we'll be able to look back and say, "He *did* lead me! Even when I wasn't aware of His guidance, He was there all along protecting me from mistakes."

God is faithful, and He knows the way through the wilderness; all we have to do is follow the ark, the presence of Christ within.

The Three Things Christians Most Want

I was sitting by a lady at a luncheon and, in response to her question, was explaining God's desire for us to live holy lives. "God doesn't ask of us something that He doesn't enable us to do, so when He says, 'Be holy as I am holy,' He makes it possible for us to do that."

"Oh—you mean He doesn't set us up to fail?"

How true! As Augustine said, "What God commands, He provides." In studying about the ark of the covenant, we see His perfect provision for holy living.

1. What were the three sacred articles inside the ark of the covenant, according to Heb. 9:4?

The manna, the budding rod, and the Ten Commandments represent the three things all true Christians desire in their spiritual lives.[2] They also describe our spiritual lives when Christ is formed within us.

The manna, discussed in chapter 5, spoke of the satisfying communion we have with God. Aaron's rod that budded represents the authority we have through Jesus, which was discussed in chapter 6.

The Ten Commandments in the ark represent for us as Christians the most wonderful promise in the Bible. The ark of the covenant was frequently called the "ark of the Testimony" (Exod. 26:33-34), because its main purpose was to hold the Law—God's testimony against sin.

God gave the Israelites laws, and they responded, "Everything the LORD has said we will do" (Exod. 24:3).

But within days, they broke the second commandment and formed a golden calf. This began their pattern of promising to obey and then failing. The story of the Israelites is a story of one disobedience after another.

For weeks our family saw a neighbor on his knees in

his yard carefully pulling up weeds that he was convinced no weed killer could kill. One day I noticed that on the other side of the driveway from where he usually worked was another large section of this same noxious weed. His work would never be done! "What he needs is some new ground that won't grow these weeds," I decided.

Perhaps that was how God felt about the Israelites when they continued to fall into their pattern of disobedience. They needed a new heart that could produce love rather than selfish desires. Could—and would—God provide that?

2. Under the old covenant, God gave the Israelites a gracious law code for living in the land. When He wanted His people to go into Canaan, it was as though He said, "Dear children, here's what I want you to do, and I'll take you by the hand and lead you along."

What had God provided for them? See Isa. 41:10, 13; 63:11-14; and Neh. 9:19-25.

3. Heb. 8:7-11 tells us God found fault with the old covenant. What had the people failed to do?

4. Despite knowing what to do and having His Spirit to guide them, the Israelites still disobeyed. What was God to do? How could He finally get an obedient people so He could delight in them? The prophets announced that God would make a new covenant with His people. What promise did God make repeatedly in the Old Testament?

Jer. 31:31-33

Ezek. 11:19

Ezek. 36:26

5. The heart of stone would have reminded the Israelites of the tables of stone. God's word had been written on tables of stone, but now His word would be in their hearts. What is significant about having His law in our minds and written on our hearts? Consider Ps. 40:7-8.

Many people are living under the old covenant. They receive His Word and respond, "Yes, we'll do whatever You want us to do." Later they find that their desires are contrary to what God wants and may even feel powerless to obey. They're sorry. They seek His forgiveness and again set out to do His will.

6. Eventually they could agree with Paul: "What a wretched man I am! Who will rescue me from this body of death?" How did Paul answer his own question in Rom. 7:24—8:4?

The new covenant provides something better—a heart delighting in God's will.

7. One wife received a daily list of chores her husband wanted her to do—cleaning, errands, cooking. Every morning he would remind her of this list, and at night he would check to see if she had completed her tasks.

She dutifully completed each task, knowing she would face trouble if she didn't. Eventually the husband died, and she remarried.

One day she was rummaging through a drawer and found an old list. When she read it, she thought, "Wow! I'm still doing every one of those things—not because I have to, but because I love to please my husband!"

That's how it is under the new covenant. With His law in our hearts, it's as natural for us to want to obey Him as it is for the birds to fly. Even under the old covenant, God was seeking a loving relationship with His people. Unlike with the demanding husband, His laws were always for their benefit. But not until God puts His law within us do we want to express our love to Him in everything we do.

What is the result of loving the Lord, according to John 14:15, 23?

Look to Him who promised to remove that stony heart that says, "I want my way!" He who is the author and finisher of our faith says, "Be holy, because I am holy" (Lev. 11:44). When we believe that He who promised to put His law within our hearts is faithful, we are made holy.

8. Having His law in our hearts doesn't mean we don't want to have things pleasant, to have a life of ease, or to have others think well of us; but when a choice between pleasing self and pleasing God must be made, we respond to the desire to please God. Even Jesus had natural desires, but He chose to submit. See Luke 22:42.

We're made holy not by keeping the law, but by trusting Jesus to keep the law within us. We just learn to rest in Him, to respond to His guidance, to use His strength, and to have His joy. Then Christ fills our spirits.

With His law in our hearts we are free to live only for His glory!

Memorize: God has chosen to make known among the Gentiles the glorious riches of this mystery, which is Christ in you, the hope of glory *(Col. 1:27).*

Prayer: *Dear Lord, You have put Your law within my heart. That "I want my own way" attitude has been replaced by a yielded heart that says, "Not my will, but Yours." In my heart You have found Your resting-place.*

Thank You for calling me to live a holy life and then for making perfect provision for me to do so. I have trusted You for cleansing, and You have given me the heart that seeks only to please You. I give You praise in Jesus' name. Amen.

Those who have a passion for His glory also have a passion for His holiness in their lives.

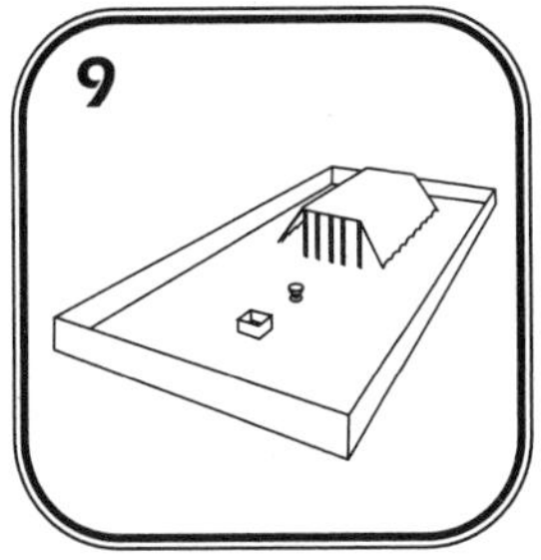

Are You All for His Glory?

ALL the furniture in both the holy place and the most holy place was made either of pure gold or gold-plated acacia wood. When the high priest entered, he saw only gold. No acacia wood was showing.

Fulfilled in Christ

Christ was both God and man. Gold speaks of His divinity or righteousness, and the acacia wood suggests His perfect humanity. In Isa. 53:2, He was referred to as "a root out of dry ground."

Because Jesus was sinless, He never sought to be the one noticed. His desire was always that His Father be the One others saw. "I did not speak of my own accord, but the Father who sent me commanded me what to say and how to say it. . . . So whatever I say is just what the Father has told me to say" (John 12:49-50). Rather than seeking prominence for himself, He only cared that He obeyed His Father. "Father, glorify your name!" (v. 28), He prayed.

His willingness to humble himself—to have the acacia wood hidden by the gold—is our example of how to prepare ourselves to be God's dwelling.

Fulfilled in Us

How significant it is that there was no acacia wood apparent in God's holy dwelling! When we are patterned after the Tabernacle, our flesh, or acacia wood, is to be covered. If our acacia wood is showing, then we have not prepared our spirits according to the pattern given on the mount. God does not recognize us as His dwelling place if we're not willing to humbly desire that others see only Christ in our lives. Instead, He sees a carnal desire for another's praise, admiration, attention. God comes to cleanse us of those desires unlike Christ so we can be filled with His glory.

When our deepest desire is to give God glory, our fleshly ambition for personal recognition and prominence no longer motivates us. God looks down and sees an attitude within us that says, "God, as long as You're glorified, it's unimportant whether others notice me or if another is promoted instead of me." God is pleased to live in such a dwelling.

In a few days our daughter Arla and her husband, Kris, will move into their new home. The morning before the movers arrive, her mother-in-law and I will help Arla clean in preparation for the arrival of their furniture.

A much greater One has said He is coming to His home. The King in His glory is coming to dwell within our hearts, and He anticipates some preparation.

> "In the desert prepare the way for the LORD; make straight in the wilderness a highway for our God. Every valley shall be raised up, every mountain and hill made low; the rough ground shall become level, the rugged places a plain. And the glory of the LORD will be revealed."
>
> —Isa. 40:3-5

The valleys and mountains leveled would require divine action, but the people were responsible to prepare the highway of holiness for their coming King.

> "Build up, build up, prepare the road! Remove the obstacles out of the way of my people." For this is

> what the high and lofty One says—he who lives forever, whose name is holy: "I live in a high and holy place."
>
> —Isa. 57:14-15

John the Baptist, of whom Isaiah prophesied, "Prepare the way for the Lord," preached, "The ax is already at the root of the trees" (Matt. 3:3, 10). Before the King comes, He requires removal of root sins. A lady who repeatedly asked God to forgive her for gossiping was told, "It's good you ask for forgiveness, but you need to pray for cleansing from the attitude that causes you to want to gossip."

God can remove root problems, but He asks that we do our part by admitting and confessing any obstacle to His indwelling. When Paul says, "Let us purify ourselves" (2 Cor. 7:1), he is speaking of our responsibility to allow His Spirit to search our hearts and expose what does not please Him.

Is Your Acacia Wood Showing?

If we have a passion for His glory, we have a passion to know our own hearts. "I will not yield my glory to another," God warns in Isa. 48:11. If we want to take the glory ourselves, His power and His glory will not rest on us.

"All my longings lie open before you, O Lord" (Ps. 38:9). To help you prepare for His presence, let God search your heart through the following questions.

1. *Is my delight in pleasing Him or in my own honor?* Our "motives are weighed by the LORD" (Prov. 16:2). To the degree that we have the mind of Christ, we, too, will weigh our motives. Our natural mind might say, "I wonder if others are impressed." The mind of Christ asks, "Am I doing this to please God?" If we know He is pleased, we are satisfied.

In John 12 the leaders failed to confess their faith because they were afraid of being put out of the synagogue.

Verse 43 states, "They loved praise from men more than praise from God."

How do you think they would have responded if they had been asked, "Why is it that you refused to obey the Lord totally?" They probably would not have given God's analysis and said, "I loved praise from men more than praise from God." What other reasons might they have found to be more acceptable to their own consciences?

If our desire is to give God glory, our cause for rejoicing is in knowing He is pleased. What were the causes for rejoicing in Acts 5:41; 2 Cor. 12:9-10; and Phil. 1:17-18? Why do you think they could rejoice for those reasons?

2. *Does my joy depend upon success in numbers, another's admiration, public recognition, or money earned?* God is looking for those who care about nothing except opportunities for giving Him glory. What was Paul's focused concern in 1 Cor. 2:1-2 that indicated his desire was to please God and not people? What were the results of his ministry? See verses 3-5.

In my first published magazine article the editor accidentally omitted my name as author. At first I was disappointed, but then I said, "I did this for You, God, so it's OK." And it was.

Paul tells us in Phil. 2 that Jesus "did not consider equality with God something to be grasped" (v. 6). "Equality with God" for us could represent an elevated position or special prominence. What attitudes did He have that will cause every tongue to give glory to the Father? See verses 6-11.

3. *Do I have rest from selfish ambition?* Am I just as happy when another person succeeds as when I succeed? One day while I was telling the Lord that my highest joy is in pleasing Him, the Holy Spirit said, "If your highest joy is in pleasing Me, then you are just as happy when another's ministry is successful as when your own is."

I knew exactly what He meant. I had been invited to present a workshop at a conference on the West Coast in which the keynote speaker was a famous author. My first books had just come out, and I was not excited about having my small book table beside her large book table.

After the Holy Spirit spoke to me, I thought about the women buying her books and receiving spiritual help from them. I was filled with joy. I realized my joy at my book table would not depend upon personal success but upon my eagerness for God to receive glory.

In James 3:14-16, what does James say is the result of selfish ambition? Why do you think this would be true?

4. *Am I most grieved when I realize I've disobeyed Him?* Or am I more disappointed when I've been offended or humiliated, or when my goals aren't reached?

Jim said, "Whenever anything bad happened in our family, my parents would say, 'What will the people at church think?'—not 'Is this pleasing to the Lord?'" Today Jim is following his parents' footsteps. He saw them seek their peers' approval. So does he. Unfortunately, his peers don't love the Lord.

Jesus promised, "My Father will honor the one who serves me" (John 12:26). Whose honor do you think others in your family would believe you're seeking?

5. *Am I more alive to pleasing God or to the praise of others?* Paul said, "I am crucified with Christ" (Gal. 2:20, KJV). List several things a dead person doesn't do that would apply to those who are dead to carnal desires. For instance, a dead person doesn't care about being noticed or ignored; neither does one who is dead to carnal desires.

6. *Is my spirit humble and contrite?* In Isa. 57:15 God says He is pleased to dwell with these qualities. Why do you think God is attracted to such attitudes in us?

In John 3:29 John the Baptist spoke of His joy because Jesus had come. In verse 30, what was his response to Jesus' coming?

This is always our response when we come into His presence. We want to become less and to allow Him to become greater.

I realized I had missed God's direction in a particular situation and wondered why I had not been more aware of what He wanted. I wrote out the scenario, and when I reached a certain point, the Holy Spirit said, "Didn't you want to impress those women?" I saw why I couldn't hear His voice. I had had the wrong motive. What a lesson that has been to me!

7. *Do I look for opportunities to exalt myself?* Hezekiah was an exemplary king. He "trusted in the LORD" and "succeeded in everything he undertook" (2 Kings 18:5; 2 Chron. 32:30). But then "God left him to test him and to know everything that was in his heart" (2 Chron. 32:31).

The Babylonians came to Hezekiah to hear more about his miraculous healing. But rather than simply telling them of God's great miracle, Hezekiah tried to impress them with his wealth. According to Isa. 39:2, exactly what did he do?

Hezekiah did not recognize this as a test until Isaiah told him that future generations would feel the results of his pride (vv. 3-7). The trial revealed pride in his heart. How are we tested, according to Prov. 27:21?

Why do you think an opportunity to receive praise tells what is in our hearts?

Seth Rees wrote, "God lets us catch a few fish, and we burn incense to the nets. We fail to give Him the glory." What are some of the areas in which people are prone to take credit that belongs to God?

8. *Can I say, "All my desire is for You, Lord"?* "All my fountains are in you," the psalmist wrote in 87:7. Caleb could enter Canaan because he followed God wholeheartedly. As an added benefit, his descendants would also inherit it. See Num. 14:24.

A missionary to China who understands the importance of wholeheartedly following the Lord said he has often told his 13-year-old son, "If you grow up to be a garbage collector and love Jesus Christ with your whole heart, I will be very happy; but if you grow up to be a great leader or someone 'rich and famous' who serves Christ with only half a heart, I will weep over your condition."

"I will give them singleness of heart and action, so that they will always fear me for their own good and the good of their children after them" (Jer. 32:39). What does it mean to have "singleness of heart and action"?

Why are children affected if we don't have singleness of heart and action?

We want what David prayed for his son Solomon, who would build the dwelling place for God. Write the key phrase from his prayer in 1 Chron. 29:19.

9. *Am I willing for my plans for greatness to amount to nothing?* Jesus knew the price He must pay for God's approval: "I tell you the truth, unless a kernel of wheat falls to the ground and dies, it remains only a single seed. But if it dies, it produces many seeds" (John 12:24).

He was willing to be as a grain of wheat, which has no control over itself. The planter controls what happens to the grain. Think of your dreams, your goals, your deepest longing. What if God said, "Let go. Let it fall"? Can you do that at this moment?

Søren Kierkegaard titled one of his books *Purity of Heart Is to Will One Thing.* Our hearts are pure when all pretense, masks, and hidden agendas are stripped away. If in this lesson you have discovered some unsightly acacia wood, trust God to cleanse all that you confess to Him. He will equip you to be all for His glory!

Memorize: How can you believe if you accept praise from one another, yet make no effort to obtain the praise that comes from the only God? *(John 5:44).*

Prayer: *Teach me, dear Lord, to live only to glorify You. Search me, know my thoughts, show me if there is any wicked way in me. I have become hungry to know Your presence and Your power in a fresh way. All my requests can be summed up with this plea: Be glorified in my life. Be at rest in me. I want my spirit to be a place that You recognize as Your holy dwelling. In faith I pray in Jesus' name. Amen.*

As soon as Moses fully prepared the Tabernacle, God's glory filled it. God is still eager to fill us with His glory when He sees that our hearts are fully prepared through faith and obedience.

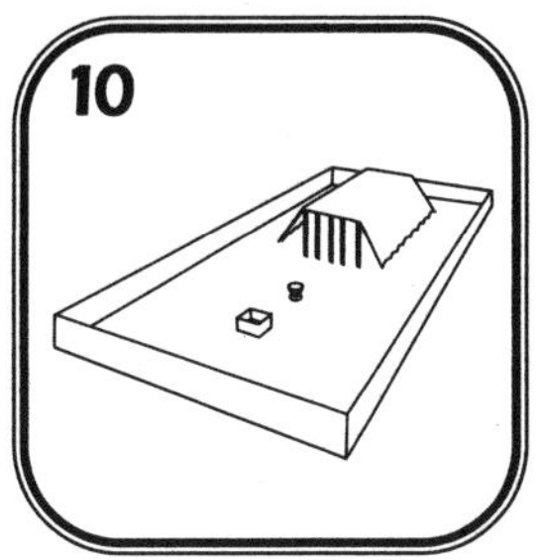

Filled with His Glory

INSIDE the holy place and the holy of holies, all the furniture was either pure gold or covered with gold. To the high priest who entered, it must have looked as if the Tabernacle were filled with gold.

Fulfilled in Christ

Christ was both God and man. The acacia wood speaks of His humanity. The gold speaks of Christ's divine righteousness.[1] "Christ is the end of the law so that there may be righteousness for everyone who believes" (Rom. 10:4).

Fulfilled in Us

God promised to give the Israelites the land of Canaan, a land where they would overcome all their enemies and find complete satisfaction. The writer to the Hebrews compares their entering into Canaan to our entering into our Sabbath rest. Sabbath rest is freedom from the struggle resulting from a divided heart. Part of us wants to please God, but another part of us wants to please self. God calls the end of that struggle a "rest." How true! When we're "in Him," we're in Canaan, the land of rest.

The Israelites sent 12 men ahead to scout out Canaan. "It is a good land," 10 of the spies admitted upon return, "but the people who live there are powerful. . . . They are stronger than we are" (Deut. 1:25; Num. 13:28, 31). They were saying in effect, "It's foolish to think we could live in that land of abundance and have constant victory."

The report of these 10 men sounds much like the reaction of those who hear God's call to be holy and say that it's foolish to consider that we could actually live a holy life.

The majority listened to the 10 spies, and the writer to the Hebrews reflected, "So we see that they were not able to enter, because of their unbelief" (3:19). It wasn't because they couldn't enter—but because they lacked faith.

The very attitude that hindered the Israelites from entering their Promised Land hinders millions today. They refuse to believe it's possible.

There was another report, though. Caleb and Joshua announced that indeed they *could* take the land. They said, "If the LORD is pleased with us, he will lead us into that land, a land flowing with milk and honey, and will give it to us. Only do not rebel against the LORD" (Num. 14:8-9). They had a spirit of faith and wholeheartedly followed the Lord (see v. 24).

In this study, we'll look at the gold that filled the Tabernacle. It speaks of the reason many Christians fail to enter the land of Canaan and why they don't experience the joy of His indwelling presence.

Draw Near in Fullness of Faith

1. We cannot overstate the significance of the gold in the Tabernacle. It was all the high priest saw on the furniture when he entered. What does the gold, which stood for Christ's divine righteousness, signify for us? If we as His dwelling are to be covered with righteousness, is our own righteousness an appropriate covering? See Isa. 64:6.

2. What did God count as righteousness in Abraham? See Gen. 15:6 and Rom. 4:2-3, 13.

3. "This righteousness from God comes through faith in Jesus Christ to all who believe" (Rom. 3:22). This truth is throughout the New Testament. Write the phrases from the following verses that indicate that our righteousness is by faith. These are only a few of the verses that state this truth.

John 16:8-10

Rom. 9:30

Phil. 3:9

2 Tim. 4:7-8

Heb. 11:7

Peter says our faith is more precious to God than gold (1 Pet. 1:7). God is not looking for those who try harder to keep the law, but for those who put more faith in His promises.

4. Just as God's glory would not have come to the Tabernacle if the acacia wood had been showing, so God does not indwell us if we're not fully trusting Him.

What role does Paul place upon faith in the following verses?

Acts 15:9

Gal. 2:20

Gal. 3:14, 22-23

5. How does God dwell in our hearts, according to Eph. 3:16-17?

"Let us draw near to God with a sincere heart in full assurance of faith" (Heb. 10:22). Nothing will welcome His glory into your spirit more than "full assurance of faith."

Hannah Whitall Smith said she had longed for complete obedience to God's will and unhindered communion with Him. She was almost ready to despair because none of her resolutions or prayers brought her the rest she desired.

Then she met some who "declared that they had discovered a 'way of holiness' wherein the redeemed soul might live and walk in abiding peace, and might be made 'more than conqueror,' through the Lord Jesus Christ." She asked them their secret, and they replied, "It is simply in ceasing from all efforts of our own and in trusting the Lord to make us holy."[2]

"Now we who have believed enter that rest. . . . For anyone who enters God's rest also rests from his own work" (Heb. 4:3, 10).

6. The only work God asks of us is faith. "God's work . . . is by faith" (1 Tim. 1:4). In John 6:29, what did Jesus say we must do to do the works of God?

7. On what does His pleasure in us depend? See Heb. 11:6.

Charles Carter calls unbelief the one basic taproot sin from which all other sins spring. Even though some earlier theologians regarded pride as the basic sin, "careful examination seems to reveal that pride itself is born of unbelief."[3] The taproot sin of a divided heart is unbelief.

8. "Never speak or think of unbelief as a weakness, but always as the sin of sins, the fruitful mother of all sin," Andrew Murray wrote.[4] Jesus shed His blood to take away all sin, and we deny the power in that Blood through unbelief. See Heb. 13:12.

9. Jesus gave one condition in which faith is impossible. "How can you believe, when you receive glory from one another, and you do not seek the glory that is from the one and only God?" (John 5:44, NASB). It's not possible to have faith if we want self to be seen. Obviously acacia wood is not visible when gold covers it.

Faith is possible, though, when we ask, "God, are You pleased?" When our whole hearts seek His approval, we find we can trust Him to work His will in our lives. What is His will for your life, according to 1 Thess. 4:3, KJV?

The word "sanctification" means "holy" or "separated wholly to God." It is His will that you be cleansed of any desires that keep you from loving God with your whole heart.

10. God made many promises, but only His promise to send the Holy Spirit to live within us was called "the promise of the Father" (Acts 1:4, KJV). Why did the Israelites fail to believe the promise God gave them, according to Heb. 4:2?

11. He invites us to "draw near to God" (Heb. 7:19), and God's love is not satisfied unless through faith we come close to Him. Because He is so eager for us to be near Him, it's not a small thing to God when we don't trust in His deliverance. See Ps. 78:18-22; Deut. 9:23; and Heb. 3:17-19.

Reflect on God's disappointment expressed in these words: "So we see that they were not able to enter, because of their unbelief" (Heb. 3:19).

12. It is possible to reach a place of rest like the bird that, above the clouds, stretches out its wings and floats on the current. What is the secret to this wonderful life? See Heb. 4:3.

Good works and our efforts are not enough; we just learn to rest in Him, respond to His guidance, use His strength, have His joy, and God's holiness fills our spirits.

"The LORD himself will establish a house for you" (2 Sam. 7:11). It is not our striving to be righteous that fills us with His glory. It is His doing in response to our faith and obedience.

13. The biblical prayers for purity assume that a pure heart is not something we can attain simply through our efforts. God creates the clean heart. See Ps. 51:7, 10.

"Let us honor the blood of the Lamb by believing that it gives the power for a life in the Holiest."[5] The instant God sees that we come to Him believing in His power to cleanse us and that He does it now, "the blood of Jesus, his Son, purifies us from all sin" (1 John 1:7).

Faith is the New Testament reality for the Old Testament symbol of pure gold. We are prepared for His indwelling when our spirits are fully trusting God.

His Glory Shall Be Revealed

If Peter had not told us that the coming of the Holy Spirit on the Day of Pentecost fulfilled Joel's prophecy, we might have thought those wonderful Old Testament prophecies referred to some still-future day.

But once Peter experienced the outpouring of the Holy Spirit, he exclaimed, "This is what was spoken by the prophet Joel: 'In the last days, God says, I will pour out my Spirit on all people'" (Acts 2:16-17; see Joel 2:28).

He could have added, "And this is what was spoken by the prophet Isaiah: 'The desert and the parched land will be glad. . . . Like the crocus, it will burst into bloom; it will rejoice greatly and shout for joy. . . . They will see the glory of the LORD'" (Isa. 35:1-2).

At last they would have relief from spiritual dryness! Areas that had been unfruitful would bear much fruit. The great joy would arrive suddenly!

"Shout and be glad, O Daughter of Zion. For I am coming, and I will live among you" (Zech. 2:10). Even in *anticipation* of His coming, they were to shout for joy. Consider what it is to actually *have* Him dwelling within!

1. The following Old Testament promises find their initial fulfillment through the coming of the Holy Spirit. What does their spiritual fulfillment mean in our lives when He comes?

Isa. 35:5

Ezek. 36:25-27

Mal. 4:2

2. When He comes, our lives change. For instance, when the Spirit fills our lives, besides the overflow of blessings, He brings a stabilizing force, a keeping power that holds us steady during storms. The framework of the Tabernacle had a board that went right through the heart of each board, so the structure was extremely sturdy—much sturdier than it might have looked on the outside. That board represents the keeping power in us when we let the Holy Spirit fully possess us.

A complete surrender to God with the resultant infilling of the Holy Spirit will change us from a state of uncertainty to one of victory and joy. Notice the strengthening promised in Isa. 35:3.

3. "You are my servant . . . in whom I will display my splendor" (Isa. 49:3). This is the promise of our Lord when He said, "You will receive power when the Holy Spirit comes on you" (Acts 1:8).[6] Write three words you think characterize the lives of those filled with God's glory.

God Enters His Dwelling Place

1. God filled the Tabernacle with His glory when all was prepared exactly as He had commanded Moses.

Though that was glorious, it was only a shadow cast by the reality of God's true desire: "The Lord has chosen Zion, he has desired it for his dwelling: 'This is my resting place for ever and ever; here I will sit enthroned, for I have desired it'" (Ps. 132:13-14). Write these verses, inserting your name in place of "Zion." (In Christian thought, Zion refers to the Church, as noted before.)

2. When the Tabernacle and the Temple of the Lord were completed, what happened? Read Exod. 40:33-35 and 2 Chron. 5:13-14, and imagine the awesomeness of a Temple filled with the weight of God's presence. (The fundamental idea of "glory" in the Old Testament is that of weight.)

3. The cloud that had been guiding and protecting the Israelites (Exod. 13:21-22) now filled the dwelling with God's holy presence. Compare this to the promise Jesus made concerning the Holy Spirit in John 14:17.

4. God always responds to our faith (gold) and obedience (covered acacia wood) by sending His glory. When the way is prepared for Him to enter His dwelling, celebration is in order! Notice the words of joyous anticipation in Ps. 24:9-10.

My friend Nancy is coming to see me, and I intend to clean house before she arrives. But a clean house will not give me the joy of her presence. When she arrives, I will open the door and expect her to come in.

God says, "Prepare me a dwelling place. Remove the obstacles of rebellion and pride, but then open the door. Believe, and you will receive 'the sanctifying work of the Spirit'" (1 Pet. 1:2). God will know He is welcomed when He sees your faith, which is more precious to Him than the gold that filled the Tabernacle (v. 7).

"'Then suddenly the Lord you are seeking will come to his temple; the messenger of the covenant, whom you desire, will come,' says the LORD Almighty" (Mal. 3:1).

At last His promise is fulfilled: "Then have them make a sanctuary for me, and I will dwell among them" (Exod. 25:8).

5. Write His words of blessing to you in Isa. 60:1-2.

Memorize: Though you have not seen him, you love him; and even though you do not see him now, you believe in him and are filled with an inexpressible and glorious joy *(1 Pet. 1:8).*

Prayer: *Dear Lord, from this moment I am all for Your glory. If You are glorified, I am satisfied. Thank You for the joy of Your presence. I praise You in the name of Jesus, who shed His blood that I might be cleansed from all sin. Amen.*

APPENDIX

Suggestions for Leaders

WHY did God speak of spiritual concepts in symbols—things we can see, touch, smell, hear? He wants us to understand the reality of the spiritual. God has always sought those who worship with their spirits.

"These are a shadow of the things that were to come; the reality, however, is found in Christ" (Col. 2:17). Reality is the spiritual life of Christ within us.

The Bible's word pictures teach profound truths. For instance, Rom. 5:14 says that Adam was a pattern of the one to come; 1 Cor. 10:4 tells us the rock in Exod. 17:6 refers to Christ.

The Tabernacle is another symbol (Heb. 8:5). "These things . . . were written down . . . for us, on whom the fulfillment of the ages has come" (1 Cor. 10:11). In fact, "Everything that was written in the past was written to teach us" (Rom. 15:4).

The Lord reveals the most to those who love Him the most. "I love those who love me, and those who seek me find me" (Prov. 8:17). We seek new understanding, not to fill our notebooks or to appear knowledgeable, but because our spirits want to know Him, to experience Him. Our seeking then becomes an act of love much as two lovers who want to learn about each other. Lovers aren't seeking knowledge so they can report to someone what they've learned; they simply aren't satisfied without knowing. God delights in revealing himself to us when He sees we long to know Him.

Additional Chapter Comments

Chapter 1

An interest in spirituality is perhaps the fastest-growing trend in North America. Fifty percent of the titles on the best-seller lists deal with such issues as spirituality, personal growth, and alternative health.[1] Twenty years ago many of these books would not have been taken seriously. Today they are becoming mainstream.

Despite this interest in spirituality, unless the Holy Spirit is within us, our spirits are empty. We remain unsatisfied and spiritually dead. The highest that God has to offer us is the gift of His Spirit to indwell our spirits. The purpose of this book is to instill a love for this priceless gift.

"Then have them make a sanctuary for me, and I will dwell among them" (Exod. 25:8). The root meaning of the word "sanctuary" carries the thought of holiness or sacredness.

God calls us to provide a holy place where He can dwell permanently. The word "holy" is used to refer to the Tabernacle 31 times in Exodus. Even the engraving on the priest's headpiece was to read, "HOLINESS TO THE LORD" (28:36, KJV).

Chapter 2

Why couldn't Moses, the one who was a friend of God, enter the Promised Land? The children of Israel were thirsty and complained to Moses, "Why did you bring the LORD's community into this desert, that we and our livestock should die here?"

God told him to speak to the rock, and it would pour forth water. Instead, he struck the rock twice with his staff. Water gushed out, and the people and animals drank (Num. 20:4, 8-11).

But the Lord said to Moses and Aaron, "Because you did not trust in me enough to honor me as holy in the sight of the Israelites, you will not bring this community into the land I give them" (v. 12).

Why did that one act of disobedience disqualify Moses from entering the Promised Land?

God chose Moses to be a picture for us of what it means to live in His presence. God wanted to teach that we live in the land of rest only if we fully surrender to Him at every point. "If you are willing and obedient, you will eat the best from the land" (Isa. 1:19). We enter God's rest through surrender to our holy God.

To let God be God—this is the essence of holiness. A full and continual surrender yields the joys of Canaan.

Chapter 3

Those who have passed the consuming fire of the brazen altar and the cleansing of the laver have one thing in common: we desire to serve. A passion to minister to the Lord consumes us. "Lord, it doesn't matter what You want me to do—only let me do something for You" becomes our heart's cry.

Without inner cleansing, though, we cannot serve Him. "Be pure, you who carry the vessels of the LORD" (Isa. 52:11).

Paul says two types of Christians exist—the usable and the unusable: "In a wealthy home some utensils are made of gold and silver, and some are made of wood and clay. The expensive utensils are used for special occasions, and the cheap ones are for everyday use. If you keep yourself pure, you will be a utensil God can use for his purpose. Your life will be clean, and you will be ready for the Master to use you for every good work" (2 Tim. 2:20-21, NLT).

Before the cleansing we are not "zealous of good works" (Titus 2:14, KJV). But when we are purified of double-mindedness, (James 4:8), we are prepared to serve with our whole hearts.

Chapter 4

God most often used light as a symbol of His presence. Moses first saw His presence in flames of fire in a bush (Exod. 3:2). Later God appeared as a pillar of fire (13:21). Jesus came as the Light of the World (John 8:12; 9:5), and Paul tells us God "lives in unapproachable light" (1 Tim. 6:16). Heaven "does not need the sun or the moon . . . , for the glory of God gives it light" (Rev. 21:23).

Therefore, we would expect His dwelling place to have

a light within it. More than with any other piece of furniture, God directed His people to be careful to make the lampstand according to the pattern He gave.

You may want to discuss the contrast between those who have the light Jesus gives and those who are in darkness because of unbelief. "The god of this age has blinded the minds of unbelievers, so that they cannot see the light of the gospel" (2 Cor. 4:4).

When our love for Christ increases, our discernment increases. In Phil. 1:9-10, Paul prayed that their love would "abound" so that they would "be able to discern what is best." When we begin to love Christ, we move closer to Him and can see more clearly what pleases Him.

Chapter 5

When the Israelites refused to be satisfied with manna, God allowed them to have quail. Notice in Num. 11:31-34 that the people gathered more than they could possibly eat. Every family brought home at least 10 homers, which would have been at least 10 donkey loads.

Many of them paid with their lives for this indulgence. The place was called "Graves of Craving." It would be remembered as the place where they craved so much that they got sick on it.

Does this insatiable craving seem to you to be a strange penalty for refusing to be satisfied with God's heavenly bread? Consider how people today who refuse to obey God's command want more and more and still are unsatisfied.

If we don't delight in God's Word, we become increasingly difficult to satisfy. Ronald Dahl, a professor of psychiatry and pediatrics, reports that though teens are surrounded by ever greater stimulation, their young faces look disappointed and bored. Parents shell out money for movies, camps, and visits to the mall. Still many teenagers appear apathetic and burned out, with a "been there, done that" air of indifference toward much of life.[2]

You might want to discuss how important it is that our

lives reflect our satisfaction in Christ. If we don't find satisfaction in Him, nothing satisfies us. Other stimulation must increase as we seek to gratify our spirit hunger. How might the results of our failing to be satisfied in Christ be seen in our children?

Chapter 6

Satan knows how much God enjoys meeting with us at this golden altar. How Satan tries to distract us! I begin to remember details of things I suddenly need to do, or I have to fight drowsiness. It may help us to come more joyfully and regularly if we capture the sense of being precious to God when we pray.

Our prayers must be all for His glory. The golden altar was made of acacia wood (representing our humanity) but completely covered with gold. We can't come to God offering sacrifices that are for our own selfish desires. When we want God to be glorified more than anything else, our requests are pleasing to Him.

Jesus is eager for His Father to be glorified, so He answers when we pray in His name. Prayers that He himself would ask, those prayers in perfect harmony with the Spirit of Jesus, will be answered so that the Father will receive glory.

Chapter 7

I think John wept much (Rev. 5:4) because he had a glimpse of what it means for sinful man to stand before a holy God. No greater contrast exists than that between the sorrow expressed by John's weeping and the joy expressed in the song of praise for the Lamb.

Jesus shed His blood for one reason: to enable us to live our lives near God. "A better hope is introduced, by which we draw near to God" (Heb. 7:19).

The New Testament reveals that the veil that separated the holy place from the most holy place represented the flesh of Jesus Christ that was torn for us on the Cross. When Jesus cried, "It is finished" (John 19:30), "the curtain of the temple was torn in two from top to bottom" (Matt 27:51). The way into the holy of holies was opened.

H. Orton Wiley states, "The two compartments of the Tabernacle represent two realms of service, one wrought at a distance with a veil between, the other in the full light of His countenance. . . . There are two degrees of fellowship with God, one as a sinner who has been pardoned and received into sonship, the other as a son who has fully consecrated all his redeemed powers to God."[3]

Once we are cleansed by the blood of Jesus, we can enter into the presence of God. Only the pure in heart see God.

Chapter 8

When David was eager to build a house for God, he said, "I had it in my heart to build a house as a place of rest for the ark of the covenant of the LORD, for the footstool of our God, and I made plans to build it."

But God told him, "You are not to build a house for my Name, because you are a warrior and have shed blood. . . . Solomon your son is the one who will build my house" (see 1 Chron. 28:2-3, 6).

Why did being a man of war disqualify David, the man after God's own heart, to build His house? Was God punishing David for fighting God's enemies? Was this a fair decree?

Indeed it was fair, but this was not a punishment. God was allowing David to teach us this important lesson: David, the man of war who had to fight God's enemies, could not build the resting-place for God. It would be Solomon, whose name meant "rich in peace," who could build the sanctuary for God's continual presence.

Struggle was necessary for the establishment of God's kingdom then, and it still is today within us. But a time can come when that struggle is over. The inner nature that was hostile to God will then be at peace. God is saying, "Before I can indwell you, the battle against self must be ended."

Chapter 9

In John 12:21 some Greeks told one of the disciples, "Sir, we would like to see Jesus." They wanted a glimpse of this miracle worker. Read verses 20-29.

The Greeks told Philip, Philip told Andrew, and together they told Jesus. Why didn't Philip go directly to Jesus? Perhaps he hesitated because he knew Jesus wouldn't welcome the opportunity to appear as a celebrity. He never responded to people's desires to bring Him fame.

Jesus' response got to the heart of this matter. "The hour has come that the Son of Man should be glorified," He said (v. 23, NKJV). It was as though He said, "Yes, I'm about to receive glory, but it won't be from the Greeks." He sought the glory that would come from God alone.

If Jesus had responded as many do today, He might have said this would "promote the cause" or "widen His influence." But God knows those whose efforts are all for His glory.

Chapter 10

In so many ways God tells us that faith is the condition for receiving His presence. Before the high priest could enter the holy of holies, he had to wash himself and put on a linen garment. This is a beautiful picture of how we prepare to enter into God's presence. We must be washed by the Word, then be covered by linen.

"Weave the tunic of fine linen and make the turban of fine linen" (Exod. 28:39). God doesn't leave it to the imagination to know what linen represents for us as God's saints. "Fine linen stands for the righteous acts of the saints" (Rev. 19:8).

Yet, as we know from Isa. 64:6, our righteousness is as filthy rags and would never be a fitting garment in which to appear before Christ. Faith is what God counts as righteousness, both for us and for Abraham.

Through faith we enter into His presence, and through faith we prepare ourselves for Him to live in us.

Notes

Preface

1. Thomas Ralston, *Elements of Divinity* (Salem, Ohio: H. E. Schmul, 1971), 199.

Introduction

1. Clarence W. Hall, *Samuel Logan Brengle: Portrait of a Prophet* (Chicago: Salvation Army Supply and Purchasing Dept., 1933), 225.

Chapter 1

1. C. S. Lewis, *Prince Caspian,* Book 2 of *The Chronicles of Narnia* (New York: Collier Books, 1977), 147.
2. William Dyrness, *Themes in Old Testament Theology* (Downers Grove, Ill.: InterVarsity Press, 1979), 37.
3. C. S. Lewis, *The Last Battle,* Book 7 of *The Chronicles of Narnia* (New York: Collier Books, 1977), 169.
4. *The Wesley Bible* (Nashville: Thomas Nelson Publishers, 1990), 889.

Chapter 2

1. *Encyclopedia Judaica* (Jerusalem: Keter Publishing House, 1971), 15:683.
2. William M. Greathouse, *Love Made Perfect: Foundations for the Holy Life* (Kansas City: Beacon Hill Press of Kansas City, 1997), 38.
3. H. Orton Wiley, *The Epistle to the Hebrews,* ed. Morris A. Weigelt (Kansas City: Beacon Hill Press of Kansas City, 1984), 296.

Chapter 3

1. *Matthew Henry's Commentary* (Iowa Falls, Iowa: World Bible Publishers, n.d.), 5:1162.
2. "Asteroid Scare Provokes Soul-Searching," *Science* 279 (Mar. 20, 1998): 1843.

Chapter 4

1. Adam Clarke, *Clarke's Commentary* (New York: Abingdon Press, n.d.), 6:986.

Chapter 5

1. William Barclay, *The Gospel of Luke,* in Daily Study Bible Series (Philadelphia: Westminster Press, 1975), 264.

2. David Stern, *Jewish New Testament Commentary* (Clarksville, Md.: Jewish New Testament Publications, 1995), 174.

3. Ibid., 931.

Chapter 6

1. A. B. Simpson, *Christ in the Tabernacle* (Harrisburg, Pa.: Christian Publications, n.d.), 106.

2. C. H. Spurgeon, *The Treasury of David,* vol. 3a (Grand Rapids: Zondervan Publishing House, 1976), 460.

3. C. S. Lewis, "Reflections on the Psalms," in *The Inspirational Writings of C. S. Lewis* (New York: Inspirational Press, 1994), 178-79.

Chapter 7

1. Clarence Larkin, *The Book of Revelation* (Philadelphia: Erwin W. Moyer Co., 1919), 45.

Chapter 8

1. John Piper, *The Pleasures of God* (Portland, Oreg.: Multnomah Press, 1991), 23.

2. Wiley, *Epistle to the Hebrews,* 254.

Chapter 10

1. Stephen Olford, *The Tabernacle: Camping with God* (Neptune, N.J.: Loizeaux Brothers, 1971), 18.

2. A. M. Hills, *Holiness and Power* (Salem, Ohio: Schmul Publishing Co., 1988), 218.

3. Charles Webb Carter, *The Person and Ministry of the Holy Spirit* (Grand Rapids: Baker Book House, 1974), 140.

4. Andrew Murray, *The Holiest of All* (Grand Rapids: Fleming H. Revell Co., 1997), 150.

5. Ibid., 330.

6. Wiley, *Epistle to the Hebrews,* 267.

Appendix

1. James Berry, *The Edge* (n.p., 1997), 24.

2. Ronald Dahl, "Burned Out and Bored," *Newsweek,* Dec. 15, 1998, 18.

3. Wiley, *Epistle to the Hebrews,* 255.

More from Aletha Hinthorn . . .

THE SATISFIED HEART TOPICAL BIBLE STUDY SERIES

BOLDLY ASKING

Deepening your walk with God through prayer

ALETHA HINTHORN

Discover what it means to come boldly to God in joyous praise, to bring requests, and to expect the abundance of life devoted to unhindered prayer.

BF083-411-6057

JOYFULLY FOLLOWING

Deepening your walk with God through joy

ALETHA HINTHORN

Add depth to your Christian walk through the joy and absolute necessity of following the Lord in wholehearted obedience.

BF083-411-6065

QUIETLY RESTING

Deepening your walk with God through rest

ALETHA HINTHORN

Discover the peace that passes all understanding and the rest that God gives as a natural result of the truly Spirit-filled life.

BF083-411-6073

SIMPLY TRUSTING

Deepening your walk with God through faith

ALETHA HINTHORN

Simply Trusting will guide you in deepening your faith and living with the confidence that God will answer your prayers.

BF083-411-6049

To order, or for a free catalog featuring other popular Beacon Hill Bible Studies, call 1-800-877-0700. www.bhillkc.com